THOMAS CARLYLE

AN ESSAY ON BURNS

BY

THOMAS CARLYLE

WITH SELECTED POEMS BY BURNS

EDITED WITH AN INTRODUCTION AND NOTES BY JULIAN W. ABERNETHY, Ph.D., FORMERLY PRINCIPAL OF BERKELEY INSTITUTE, BROOKLYN

WILDSIDE PRESS

CONTENTS

	PAGE
INTRODUCTION	5
THOMAS CARLYLE	5
ROBERT BURNS	10
BIBLIOGRAPHY	16
ESSAY ON BURNS	19
POEMS OF BURNS	103
TO A MOUSE	103
TO A MOUNTAIN DAISY	105
HIGHLAND MARY	107
YE BANKS AND BRAES	108
MY LUVE'S LIKE A RED, RED ROSE	109
O, WERT THOU IN THE CAULD BLAST	110
SCOTS WHA HAE	110
AULD LANG SYNE	111
NOTES	113
TOPICS FOR STUDY AND DISCUSSION	130
GLOSSARY	133

INTRODUCTION

THOMAS CARLYLE

THOMAS CARLYLE, the "Seer of Chelsea" and the "Censor of the Age," was born at Ecclefechan, near Annan, Scotland, in 1795. His father was a stone-mason and small farmer; his mother learned late in life to use a pen, that she might write to her son Thomas. His genius, like that of Burns, of whom he wrote with such sympathetic insight, sprang directly from the cold Scotch soil. At fourteen he entered the University of Edinburgh, but left after completing the ordinary course without taking a degree, owing to the University nothing, as he said bitterly, except the opportunity afforded by its library for multifarious reading. He distinguished himself, however, in the higher mathematics, and one of his first published works was a translation of Legendre's Geometry. He engaged in teaching, but soon came to "the grim conclusion that school-mastering must end, whatever pleased to follow." He next studied divinity for a time, as it was the wish of his parents that he should enter the ministry; but finally declared boldly for literature as his profession, and began his career as an author, in 1824, with a *Life of Schiller* and an admirable translation of Goethe's *Wilhelm Meister*.

In 1826 Carlyle married Jane Welsh, a lineal descendant from John Knox, and soon afterward went to reside upon her small estate of Craigenputtock, near Dumfries. Here in this "loneliest nook in Britain," as he described it, "in a wilderness of heath and rock," these wedded students—for his wife's intellectual gifts were comparable with his own—spent about six years, like Wordsworth and his sister, in "plain living and high thinking." Here he wrote the best of his critical essays, and also the remarkable work, *Sartor Resartus*, a kind of spiritual biography of himself, presenting the main features of his subsequent teaching, which first appeared in book form in America, in 1836, with an introduction by Emerson. He removed to London in 1834, and fixed his final home in Chelsea.

His masterpiece, the *History of the French Revolution*, was published in 1837. *Chartism*, a criticism upon the social condition of England, appeared in 1839; *Heroes and Hero Worship*, in 1841; *Past and Present*, in 1843; *Oliver Cromwell's Letters and Speeches*, in 1845; and *Latter-Day Pamphlets*, in 1850, a series of violent diatribes upon social questions, which at the time brought the author more credit for madness than for wisdom. The charming *Life of John Sterling* appeared in 1851, followed by his most elaborate historical work, the *Life of Frederick the Great*, from 1858 to 1865. In 1866 he was elected Lord Rector of Edinburgh University, and his Installation Address was attended by the most enthusiastic public manifestations of approval and honor. His last work was the *Early Kings of Norway*, published in 1875. He died February 5, 1881.

Carlyle's personal character was remarkable for its inflexible integrity and lofty independence. "No praise can be deemed too high for the resolute devotion with which, through evil report and good report, through poverty and riches, through obscurity and fame, he remained constantly honest to his convictions, resolved to write on no subject which he had not studied to the bottom, and determined to speak out what he believed to be the truth, however unpalatable it might be to the world." He was a profound thinker, but not a clear reasoner; he had too much of the fire of the poet to engage in dull analysis and matter-of-fact reasoning. He felt deeply, but not calmly; the activity of his nature, moral and intellectual, was tumultuous. He was a moralist rather than a philosopher.

His ethical creed was a stern, uncompromising insistence upon the performance of duty as the chief end of life. Men must not labor in hope of reward, but must recognize that they deserve nothing. The theory of life that makes happiness an end is false and contemptible. "*Would* in this world of ours is as mere zero to *should*." Of specific duties, the first and greatest is work. "Do thy little stroke of work; this is Nature's voice, and the sum of all the commandments, to each man." "Produce! Produce! Were it but the pitifulest infinitesimal fraction of a Product, produce it in God's name." The "Captains of Industry" are the only true aristocrats. Two men are to be honored, and no third, "the toil-worn Craftsman who conquers the earth, and he who is seen toiling for the spiritually indispensable." The second great duty is that of obedience. "Obedience is our universal duty and destiny; wherein whoso will not bend must break." The third great duty is veracity, or sincerity, as opposed to all cant, puffery, quackery, and sham. The greatest evils in life to be battled against are idleness, imposture, and unveracity. "Quack-ridden; in that one word lies all misery whatsoever. Speciosity in all departments usurps the place of reality." This is a literary duty also. A chief merit of Burns, he says, is his "indisputable air of reality."

"Carlyle's essays," says Professor Nicoll, "are among the most valuable of his writings. He was the first to make the great writers of Germany known in England; and his writings on the more illustrious figures of the epoch of the French Revolution—Voltaire, Diderot, Mirabeau—are models of insight into character, profound and discriminating estimates of men who had proved stumbling-blocks to British critics. The essays on Burns and Johnson may be said to have struck the keynote of all succeeding writings on these men; while his criticism of Scott, which has provoked a good deal of hostility, is more and more coming to be generally recognized as substantially correct. The *Life of Schiller*, though warmly praised by Goethe, who added a preface to the German translation of it, is not a first-rate performance. But the *Life of John Sterling* is a perfect triumph of literary art, far and away the best biography of its size in the language."

Of his literary qualities James Russell Lowell says: "The great merit of the essays lay in a criticism based on wide and various study, which, careless of tradition, applied its standard to the real and not the contemporary worth of the literary or other performance to be judged, and in an unerring eye for that fleeting expression of the moral features of character, a perception of which alone makes the drawing of a coherent likeness possible. Their defect was a tendency, gaining strength with years, to confound the moral with the æsthetic standard, and to make the value of an author's work dependent on the general force of his nature rather than on its special fitness for a given task. But, with all deductions, he remains the profoundest critic and the most dramatic imagination of modern times. His manner is not so well suited to the historian as to the essayist. He is always great in single figures and striking episodes, but there is neither gradation nor continuity. He sees history, as it were, by flashes of lightning. He makes us acquainted with the isolated spot where we happen to be when the flash comes, as if by actual eyesight, but there is no possibility of a comprehensive view. No other writer compares with him for vividness. With the gift of song, Carlyle would have been the greatest of epic poets since Homer."

Of the influence of Carlyle's writings Mr. Lowell says: "Though not the safest of guides in politics or practical philosophy, his value as an inspirer and awakener cannot be overestimated. It is a power which belongs only to the highest order of minds, for it is none but a divine fire that can so kindle and irradiate. The debt due him from those who listened to the teachings of his prime for revealing to them what sublime reserves of power even the humblest may find in manliness, sincerity, and self-reliance, can be paid with nothing short of reverential gratitude. As a purifier of the sources whence our intellectual inspiration is drawn, his influence has been second only to that of Wordsworth, if even to his.''

ROBERT BURNS

ROBERT BURNS was born January 25, 1759, in a clay cottage built by his father's own hands, which still stands by the roadside about two miles from the village of Ayr. Near by are the "Brig o' Doon" and "Alloway's auld haunted kirk," ruins that Burns's poems have made as sacred as any in Europe. His father was a hard-working farmer, intelligent, upright, and deeply religious. We know him well from the portrait reverently painted by the poet in "The Cotter's Saturday Night." The mother was a bright and cheerful woman, with a memory richly stored with old songs and ballads. When Robert was seven years old the family moved to Mt. Olivet, a poor upland farm about two miles away. Here eleven years were spent in a desperate struggle for mere existence.

There were seven children, of whom Robert was the eldest. Poverty made systematic education impossible, but some instruction was given by the father in the long winter evenings and a tutor was employed for a short time by neighboring families from whom he obtained a good discipline in English and a frail knowledge of French. There were a few good books in the home, the *Spectator*, some of the plays of Shakespeare, Pope's *Homer*, Allan Ramsay's works, and especially a collection of songs, of which Burns says: "I pored over them driving my cart or walking to labor, song by song, verse by verse."

The farm at Mt. Olivet was abandoned and the next experiment was at Lochlea, in the parish of Tarbolton. Here Burns lived until his twenty-fifth year, and here his life was broadened by town experience. To give his rustic manners a "touching up," as he said, he attended a dancing school, and a new world of social pleasures was opened to him; and there was a debating society, established by his brother Gilbert and himself. About this time he "sketched the outlines of a tragedy," he says, but this ambitious scheme did not long keep him from song-writing, which began at Lochlea. He fell upon a copy of Fergusson's *Scottish Poems*, which fired his soul with patriotic and poetic zeal, and henceforth poetry was "a darling walk for my mind."

At Lochlea the father died, leaving to his sons only a legacy of debts. The family moved to Mossgiel, another poor farm that produced only new disasters for the poet-farmer. But in spite of the discouragements of hard labor and failing crops, Burns's poetic faculty here came to a splendid fruition. During his twenty-sixth and twenty-seventh years he wrote the greater part of his finest poetry, including "The Cotter's Saturday Night," "To a Mouse," "To a Mountain Daisy," "Hallowe'en," and "The Jolly Beggars." At this time he became involved in the fierce theological controversy between the New Lights, the liberal branch of the church, and the Auld Lights, the conservative or orthodox branch, and wrote the "Twa Herds," "Holy Willie's Prayer," and the "Holy Fair." These witty, satirical poems, which made his friends both laugh and grieve, introduced a new and strange element into Scottish poetry; and there is nothing like them elsewhere in the field of English satire.

Through these long years of struggle, farming had proved an utter failure for Burns. Poetry was his consolation, and he had tasted the sweets of praise among his Ayrshire neighbors; but poetry could not buy food, nor provide a home. A crisis in his life had been reached. Moreover, his susceptible heart, which was always getting him into entanglements with the neighborhood lassies, was now in a turmoil over two love affairs, one with Mary Campbell, the

"Highland Mary" who inspired two of his most beautiful songs, the other with Jean Armour, the "Bonny Jean," whom he afterwards married.

In despair and with the hope of solving all of his problems together, he decided to leave Scotland forever, obtained the promise of a position as bookkeeper on a plantation in Jamaica, and engaged his passage thither. To pay the costs he published a collection of poems, from which he received about £20. The little volume was received with enthusiasm and rapidly spread his fame. Just as he was about to embark, word came from Edinburgh that his poems had created a sensation in the capital and that a second and larger edition would be warranted. Burns immediately set out for Edinburgh, and Scotland's poet was saved.

The visit to Edinburgh is the most celebrated episode in the life of Burns. The obscure farmer-poet was suddenly brought forth into the light of national renown. He was flattered and feasted by the great people of literary and fashionable society, philosophers, preachers, lords, and duchesses vying with one another to entertain him, or rather to be entertained by him, for he was regarded somewhat as a prodigy. But according to all accounts, Burns carried himself through this remarkable experience with modesty and good sense.

The Edinburgh edition of his poems brought to Burns a good £500. Of this wealth he gave £180 to his brother Gilbert, who continued to struggle with the farm at Mossgiel. While awaiting the next turn of his fortune, he indulged in travel for a time, visiting the south of Scotland and the northern Highlands. The visions of a more honored and affluent life that he may have had during his brief Edinburgh celebrity quickly fled, as he realized that his inevitable lot was cast among commonplace country folk, a realization that cost him much turbulence and bitterness of spirit. In 1788 he married Jean Armour and wrote in her praise the charming songs, "O were I on Parnassus Hill" and "I love my Jean." At Ellisland, a few miles from Dumfries, he settled and began his last disastrous experiment with farming.

The three years at Ellisland were probably the happiest period of Burns's life. He had a home which he had built himself, and pleasant neighbors who appreciated his worth. He established a parish library, attended regularly the parish church, and in the manner of his father gathered his family every evening for worship. His fame as a poet brought many distinguished visitors to his door. Above all he found some leisure for poetry. Here he wrote "Tam o' Shanter," "by universal assent," says the editor of the Globe edition, "the crowning glory and masterpiece of its author." And here one evening, when a sacred memory was pressing upon him, he wrote "To Mary in Heaven." And to these years belong innumerable songs, among them "John Anderson," and many others nearly as famous.

In 1791 Burns left Ellisland and removed with his family to Dumfries, where the remainder of his life was spent. To eke out the profits of the farm, he had already obtained through a friend in Edinburgh the position of excise collector, and with an addition to his salary he now depended on this office for a living. The duty of measuring casks of whisky and chasing smugglers through the moors he apparently performed well, but it was an unfortunate occupation, for it brought him too closely into company with the demon of drink, whom he could never exorcise and to whom at last he sacrificed life itself. This period at Dumfries was a sad, almost tragic decline. His best friends fell away from him, and his worst friends enticed him more and more frequently to the Globe tavern, where a huge punch bowl bearing his name to-day memorializes the midnight revels with roistering companions who were wise enough to enjoy his marvelous wit and humor, and heartless enough to lead him on to ruin. Returning from one of these tavern revels late at night through deep snow, he caught a cold from which he never fully recovered. On July 21, 1796, he died, at the age of thirty-seven.

Burns the man, weak with human frailties, was soon forgotten, but Burns the poet, invested only with the glory and mystery of genius, took his place at once and forever in the heart of his native land. Scotland honors her other authors; Burns she loves with a universal, passionate, and unremitting love.

Carlyle's *Essay on Burns* is a brilliant prose classic, but its critical estimates are not always to be accepted without qualification. His failure to appreciate "Tam o' Shanter," for example, shows the necessity of testing his judgments by comparison with others. Such comparison may be made with great profit and interest in the essays of Stevenson, Brooke, Henley, and others mentioned in the appended Bibliography. For this purpose the following brief general estimates will be serviceable:

"Of all poets," says Alexander Smith, "Burns was, perhaps, the most directly inspired. His poems did not grow—like stalactites—by the slow process of accretion; like Adam, they had no childhood—they awoke complete. Burns produced all his great effects by single strokes. In his best things there is an impetus, a hurry, which gives one the idea of boundless resource. To him a song was the occupation of a morning; his poetic epistles drive along in a fiery sleet of words and images: his 'Tam o' Shanter' was written in a day—since Bruce fought Bannockburn, the best single day's work done in Scotland."

"Mankind owes him a general debt of gratitude," says Lord Rosebery, "but the debt of Scotland is special. For Burns exalted our race, he hallowed Scotland and the Scottish tongue, his Scottish notes rang through the world, and he thus preserved the Scottish language forever; for mankind will never allow to die that idiom in which his songs and poems are enshrined." On this point of his language Emerson says: "He grew up in a rural district, speaking a *patois* unintelligible to all but natives, and he has made the Lowland Scotch a Doric dialect of fame. It is the only example in history of a language made classic by the genius of a single man." Of this national quality Edmund Gosse says: "Burns is not merely the national poet of Scotland; he is, in a certain sense, the country itself: all elements of Scotch life and manners, all peculiarities of Scotch temperament and conviction, are found embroidered somewhere or other on Burns's variegated singing-robes."

In a final summary of Burns's powers, Professor Saintsbury says: "It is true that Burns's range of subject, as distinct from that of sound, was not extremely wide. He could give a voice to passion—passion of war, passion of conviviality, passion above all of love—as none but the very greatest poets ever have given or will give it; he had also an extraordinary command of *genre* painting of all kinds, ranging from the merely descriptive and observant to the most intensely satirical. Perhaps he could only do these two things—could not be (as he certainly has not been) philosophical, deeply meditative, elaborately in command of the great possibilities of nature, political, moral, argumentative. But what an 'only' have we here! It amounts to this, that Burns could 'only' seize, could 'only' convey the charms of poetical expression to, the more primitive thought and feeling of the natural man, and that he could do this supremely."

BIBLIOGRAPHY

CARLYLE

Richard Garnett: *Life of Carlyle* (*Great Writers* Series).
John Nichol: *Life of Carlyle* (*English Men of Letters* Series).
J. A. Froude: *Life of Carlyle* and *Reminiscences of Carlyle*.
  (These books are famous, interesting, and untrustworthy.)
C. E. Norton (Editor): *Letters of Thomas Carlyle*.
Moncure D. Conway: *Carlyle*.
R. S. Craig: *The Making of Carlyle* (1908).
J. R. Lowell: *My Study Windows*.
W. C. Brownell: *Victorian Prose Masters*.
Augustine Birrell: *Obiter Dicta*, First Series.
Frederic Harrison: *Studies in Early Victorian Literature*.
John Morley: *Literary Essays* (1906).
W. S. Lilly: *Four English Humorists* ("The Humorist as Prophet").
J. C. Shairp: *Aspects of Poetry* ("Prose Poets: Thomas Carlyle").

BURNS

J. C. Shairp: *Life of Burns* (*English Men of Letters* Series).
J. S. Blackie: *Life of Burns* (*Great Writers* Series).
Alexander Smith: Introduction to Globe Edition of Burns.
W. E. Henley: Introduction to Cambridge Edition.
Robert Chambers: *Life and Works of Burns*, 4 vols. (1896).
Charles S. Dougall: *The Burns Country*.
Nathaniel Hawthorne: *Our Old Home*.
Mrs. Oliphant: *Literary History of the Nineteenth Century*, Vol. I.

BIBLIOGRAPHY

R. L. Stevenson: *Familiar Studies*.
Stopford Brooke: *Theology in the English Poets*.
William Hazlitt: *Lectures on the English Poets*.
J. C. Shairp: *Aspects of Poetry*.
Charles Kingsley: *Sir Walter Raleigh and His Times*.
A. W. Ward: *The English Poets* (Matthew Arnold's Introduction).
J. Forster: *Great Teachers*.

Poems by Fitz-Greene Halleck, Whittier, Holmes, Lowell, J. W. Parsons, and Swinburne.

BURNS

IN the modern arrangements of society, it is no uncommon thing that a man of genius must, like Butler,[1] "ask for bread[2] and receive a stone;" for, in spite of our grand maxim[3] of supply and demand, it is by no means the highest excellence that men are most forward to recognize. The inventor of a spinning-jenny[4] is pretty sure of his reward in his own day; but the writer of a true poem, like the apostle of a true religion, is nearly as sure of the contrary. We do not know whether it is not an aggravation of the injustice, that there is generally a posthumous retribution. Robert Burns, in the course of Nature, might yet have been living; but his short life was spent in toil and penury; and he died, in the prime of his manhood, miserable and neglected: and yet already a brave mausoleum[5] shines over his dust, and more than one splendid monument has been reared in other places to his fame; the street where he languished in poverty is called by his name; the highest personages in our literature have been proud to appear as his commentators and admirers; and here is the *sixth* narrative of his *Life* that has been given to the world!

Mr. Lockhart[6] thinks it necessary to apologize for

this new attempt on such a subject: but his readers, we believe, will readily acquit him; or, at worst, will censure only the performance of his task, not the choice of it. The character of Burns, indeed, is a theme that cannot easily become either trite or exhausted; and will probably gain rather than lose in its dimensions by the distance to which it is removed by Time. No man, it has been said, is a hero to his valet; and this is probably true; but the fault is at least as likely to be the valet's as the hero's. For it is certain, that to the vulgar eye few things are wonderful that are not distant. It is difficult for men to believe that the man, the mere man whom they see, may perhaps painfully feel, toiling at their side through the poor jostlings of existence, can be made of finer clay than themselves. Suppose that some dining acquaintance of Sir Thomas Lucy's[1] and neighbor of John-a-Combe's,[2] had snatched an hour or two from the preservation of his game, and written us a Life of Shakspeare! What dissertations should we not have had,—not on *Hamlet* and *The Tempest*, but on the wool-trade, and deer-stealing, and the libel and vagrant laws; and how the Poacher became a Player; and how Sir Thomas and Mr. John had Christian bowels, and did not push him to extremities! In like manner, we believe, with respect to Burns, that till the companions of his pilgrimage, the Honorable Excise Commissioners,[3] and the Gentlemen of the Caledonian Hunt,[4] and the Dumfries Aristocracy, and all the Squires and Earls, equally with the Ayr Writers,[5] and the New and Old Light Clergy,[1] whom he had to do with, shall have become invisible in the darkness of the Past, or visible only by light borrowed from *his* juxtaposition, it will be difficult to measure him by any true standard, or to estimate what he really was and did, in the eighteenth century, for his country and the world. It will be difficult, we say; but still a fair problem for literary historians; and repeated attempts will give us repeated approximations.

His former Biographers have done something, no doubt, but by no means a great deal, to assist us. Dr. Currie[2] and Mr. Walker, the principal of these writers, have both, we think, mistaken one essentially important thing: Their own and the world's true relation to their author, and the style in which it became such men to think and to speak of such a man. Dr. Currie loved the poet truly; more perhaps than he avowed to his readers, or even to himself; yet he everywhere introduces him with a certain patronizing, apologetic air; as if the polite public might think it strange and half unwarrantable that he, a man of science, a scholar and gentleman, should do such honor to a rustic. In all this, however, we readily admit that his fault was not want of love, but weakness of faith; and regret that the first and kindest of all our poet's biographers should not have seen farther, or believed more boldly what he saw. Mr. Walker offends more deeply in the same kind: and both err alike in presenting us with a detached catalogue of his several supposed attributes, virtues and vices, instead of a delineation of the resulting character as a living unity. This, however, is not painting a portrait; but gauging the length and breadth of the several features, and jotting down their dimensions in arithmetical ciphers. Nay it is not so much as that: for we are yet to learn by what arts or instruments the mind *could* be so measured and gauged.

Mr. Lockhart, we are happy to say, has avoided both these errors. He uniformly treats Burns as the high and remarkable man the public voice has now pronounced him to be: and in delineating him, he has avoided the method of separate generalities, and rather sought for characteristic incidents, habits, actions, sayings; in a word, for aspects which exhibit the whole man, as he looked and lived among his fellows. The book accordingly, with all its deficiencies, gives more insight, we think, into the true character of Burns, than any prior biography: though, being written on the very popular and condensed scheme of an article for *Constable's Miscellany*,[1] it has less depth than we could have wished and expected from a writer of such power; and contains rather more, and more multifarious, quotations than belong of right to an original production. Indeed, Mr. Lockhart's own writing is generally so good, so clear, direct and nervous, that we seldom wish to see it making place for another man's. However, the spirit of the work is throughout candid, tolerant and anxiously conciliating; compliments and praises are liberally distributed, on all hands, to great and small; and, as Mr. Morris Birkbeck[1] observes of the society in the backwoods of America, "the courtesies of polite life are never lost sight of for a moment." But there are better things than these in the volume; and we can safely testify, not only that it is easily and pleasantly read a first time, but may even be without difficulty read again.

Nevertheless, we are far from thinking that the problem of Burns's Biography has yet been adequately solved. We do not allude so much to deficiency of facts or documents,— though of these we are still every day receiving some fresh accession,— as to the limited and imperfect application of them to the great end of Biography. Our notions upon this subject may perhaps appear extravagant; but if an individual is really of consequence enough to have his life and character recorded for public remembrance, we have always been of opinion that the public ought to be made acquainted with all the inward springs and relations of his character. How did the world and man's life, from his particular position, represent themselves to his mind? How did coexisting circumstances modify him from without; how did he modify these from within? With what endeavors and what efficacy rule over them; with what resistance and what suffering sink under them? In one word, what and how produced was the effect of society on him; what and how produced was his effect on society? He who should answer these questions, in regard to any individual, would, as we believe, furnish a model of perfection in Biography. Few individuals, indeed, can deserve such a study; and many *lives* will be written, and, for the gratification of innocent curiosity, ought to be written, and read and forgotten, which are not in this sense *biographies*. But Burns, if we mistake not, is one of these few individuals; and such a study, at least with such a result, he has not yet obtained. Our own contributions to it, we are aware, can be but scanty and feeble; but we offer them with good-will, and trust they may meet with acceptance from those they are intended for.

Burns first came upon the world as a prodigy; and was, in that character, entertained by it, in the usual fashion, with loud, vague, tumultuous wonder, speedily subsiding into censure and neglect; till his early and most mournful death again awakened an enthusiasm for him, which, especially as there was now nothing to be done, and much to be spoken, has prolonged itself even to our own time. It is true, the "nine days"[1] have long since elapsed; and the very continuance of this clamor proves that Burns was no vulgar wonder. Accordingly, even in sober judgments, where, as years passed by, he has come to rest more and more exclusively on his own intrinsic merits, and may now be well-nigh shorn of that casual radiance, he appears not only as a true British poet, but as one of the most considerable British men of the eighteenth century. Let it not be objected that he did little.

ROBERT BURNS

He did much, if we consider where and how. If the work performed was small, we must remember that he had his very materials to discover; for the metal he worked in lay hid under the desert moor, where no eye but his had guessed its existence; and we may almost say, that with his own hand he had to construct the tools for fashioning it. For he found himself in deepest obscurity, without help, without instruction, without model; or with models only of the meanest sort. An educated man stands, as it were, in the midst of a boundless arsenal and magazine, filled with all the weapons and engines which man's skill has been able to devise from the earliest time; and he works, accordingly, with a strength borrowed from all past ages. How different is *his* state who stands on the outside of that storehouse, and feels that its gates must be stormed, or remain forever shut against him! His means are the commonest and rudest; the mere work done is no measure of his strength. A dwarf behind his steam-engine may remove mountains; but no dwarf will hew them down with a pickaxe; and he must be a Titan[1] that hurls them abroad with his arms.

It is in this last shape that Burns presents himself. Born in an age the most prosaic Britain had yet seen, and in a condition the most disadvantageous, where his mind, if it accomplished aught, must accomplish it under the pressure of continual bodily toil, nay of penury and desponding apprehension of the worst evils, and with no furtherance but such knowledge as dwells in a poor man's hut, and the rhymes of a Fergusson[1] or Ramsay[2] for his standard of beauty, he sinks not under all these impediments: through the fogs and darkness of that obscure region, his lynx eye discerns the true relations of the world and human life; he grows into intellectual strength, and trains himself into intellectual expertness. Impelled by the expansive movement of his own irrepressible soul, he struggles forward into the general view; and with haughty modesty lays down before us, as the fruit of his labor, a gift, which Time has now pronounced imperishable. Add to all this, that his darksome drudging childhood and youth was by far the kindliest era of his whole life; and that he died in his thirty-seventh year: and then ask, If it be strange that his poems are imperfect, and of small extent, or that his genius attained no mastery in its art? Alas, his Sun shone as through a tropical tornado; and the pale Shadow of Death eclipsed it at noon! Shrouded in such baleful vapors, the genius of Burns was never seen in clear azure splendor, enlightening the world: but some beams from it did, by fits, pierce through; and it tinted those clouds with rainbow and orient colors, into a glory and stern grandeur, which men silently gazed on with wonder and tears!

We are anxious not to exaggerate; for it is exposition rather than admiration that our readers require of us here; and yet to avoid some tendency to that side is no easy matter. We love Burns, and we pity him; and love and pity are prone to magnify. Criticism, it is sometimes thought, should be a cold business;

we are not so sure of this; but, at all events, our concern with Burns is not exclusively that of critics. True and genial as his poetry must appear, it is not chiefly as a poet, but as a man, that he interests and affects us. He was often advised to write a tragedy: time and means were not lent him for this; but through life he enacted a tragedy, and one of the deepest. We question whether the world has since witnessed so utterly sad a scene; whether Napoleon himself, left to brawl with Sir Hudson Lowe[1] and perish on his rock, "amid[2] the melancholy main," presented to the reflecting mind such a "spectacle of pity and fear" as did this intrinsically nobler, gentler and perhaps greater soul, wasting itself away in a hopeless struggle with base entanglements, which coiled closer and closer round him, till only death opened him an outlet. Conquerors are a class of men with whom, for most part, the world could well dispense; nor can the hard intellect, the unsympathizing loftiness and high but selfish enthusiasm of such persons inspire us in general with any affection; at best it may excite amazement; and their fall, like that of a pyramid, will be beheld with a certain sadness and awe. But a true Poet, a man in whose heart resides some effluence of Wisdom, some tone of the "Eternal Melodies," is the most precious gift that can be bestowed on a generation: we see in him a freer, purer development of whatever is noblest in ourselves; his life is a rich lesson to us; and we mourn his death as that of a benefactor who loved and taught us.

Such a gift had Nature, in her bounty, bestowed on us in Robert Burns; but with queenlike indifference she cast it from her hand, like a thing of no moment; and it was defaced and torn asunder, as an idle bauble, before we recognized it. To the ill-starred Burns was given the power of making man's life more venerable, but that of wisely guiding his own life was not given. Destiny,—for so in our ignorance we must speak,—his faults, the faults of others, proved too hard for him; and that spirit, which might have soared could it but have walked, soon sank to the dust, its glorious faculties trodden under foot in the blossom; and died, we may almost say, without ever having lived. And so kind and warm a soul; so full of inborn riches, of love to all living and lifeless things! How his heart flows out in sympathy over universal Nature; and in her bleakest provinces discerns a beauty and a meaning! The "Daisy" falls not unheeded under his plowshare; nor the ruined nest of that "wee, cowering, timorous beastie," cast forth, after all its provident pains, to "thole the sleety dribble and cranreuch cauld."[1] The "hoar visage" of winter delights him; he dwells with a sad and oft-returning fondness in these scenes of solemn desolation; but the voice of the tempest becomes an anthem to his ears; he loves to walk in the sounding woods, for "it raises his thoughts[2] to *Him that walketh on the wings of the wind.*" A true Poet-soul, for it needs but to be struck, and the sound it yields will be music! But observe him chiefly as he mingles with his brother men. What warm, all-comprehending fellow-feeling; what trustful, boundless love; what generous exaggeration of the object loved! His rustic friend, his nut-brown maiden, are no longer mean and homely, but a hero and a queen, whom he prizes as the paragons of Earth. The rough scenes of Scottish life, not seen by him in any Arcadian illusion,[1] but in the rude contradiction, in the smoke and soil of a too harsh reality, are still lovely to him: Poverty is indeed his companion, but Love also, and Courage; the simple feelings, the worth, the nobleness, that dwell under the straw roof, are near and venerable to his heart: and thus over the lowest provinces of man's existence he pours the glory of his own soul; and they rise, in shadow and sunshine, softened and brightened into a beauty which other eyes discern not in the highest. He has a just self-consciousness, which too often degenerates into pride; yet it is a noble pride, for defense, not for offense; no cold suspicious feeling, but a frank and social one. The Peasant Poet bears himself, we might say, like a King in exile: he is cast among the low, and feels himself equal to the highest; yet he claims no rank, that none may be disputed to him. The forward he can repel, the supercilious he can subdue; pretensions of wealth or ancestry are of no avail with him; there is a fire in that dark eye, under which the "insolence of condescension" cannot thrive. In his abasement, in his extreme need, he forgets not for a moment the majesty of Poetry and Manhood. And yet, far as he feels himself above common men, he wanders not apart from them, but mixes warmly in their interests; nay throws himself into their arms, and, as it were, entreats them to love him. It is moving to see how, in his darkest despondency, this proud being still seeks relief from friendship; unbosoms himself, often to the unworthy; and, amid tears, strains to his glowing heart a heart that knows only the name of friendship. And yet he was "quick to learn;" a man of keen vision, before whom common disguises afforded no concealment. His understanding saw through the hollowness even of accomplished deceivers; but there was a generous credulity in his heart. And so did our Peasant show himself among us; "a soul like an Æolian harp,[1] in whose strings the vulgar wind, as it passed through them, changed itself into articulate melody." And this was he for whom the world found no fitter business than quarrelling with smugglers and vintners, computing excise-dues upon tallow, and gauging ale-barrels! In such toils was that mighty Spirit sorrowfully wasted: and a hundred years may pass on, before another such is given us to waste.

All that remains of Burns, the Writings he has left, seem to us, as we hinted above, no more than a poor mutilated fraction of what was in him; brief, broken glimpses of a genius that could never show itself complete; that wanted all things for completeness: culture, leisure, true effort, nay even length of life. His poems are, with scarcely any exception, mere occasional effusions; poured forth with little premeditation; expressing, by such means as offered, the passion, opinion, or humor of the hour. Never in one instance was it permitted him to grapple with any subject with the full collection of his strength, to fuse and mold it in the concentrated fire of his genius. To try by the strict rules of Art such imperfect fragments, would be at once unprofitable and unfair. Nevertheless, there is something in these poems, marred and defective as they are, which forbids the most fastidious student of poetry to pass them by. Some sort of enduring quality they must have: for after fifty years of the wildest vicissitudes in poetic taste, they still continue to be read; nay, are read more and more eagerly, more and more extensively; and this not only by literary virtuosos, and that class upon whom transitory causes operate most strongly, but by all classes, down to the most hard, unlettered and truly natural class, who read little, and especially no poetry, except because they find pleasure in it. The grounds of so singular and wide a popularity, which extends, in a literal sense, from the palace to the hut, and over all regions where the English tongue is spoken, are well worth inquiring into. After every just deduction, it seems to imply some rare excellence in these works. What is that excellence?

To answer this question will not lead us far. The excellence of Burns is, indeed, among the rarest, whether in poetry or prose; but, at the same time, it is plain and easily recognized: his *Sincerity*, his indisputable air of Truth. Here are no fabulous woes or joys; no hollow fantastic sentimentalities; no wire-drawn refinings, either in thought or feeling: the passion that is traced before us has glowed in a living heart; the opinion he utters has risen in his own understanding, and been a light to his own steps. He does not write from hearsay, but from sight and experience; it is the scenes that he has lived and labored amidst, that he describes: those scenes, rude and humble as they are, have kindled beautiful emotions in his soul, noble thoughts, and definite resolves; and he speaks forth what is in him, not from any outward call of vanity or interest, but because his heart is too full to be silent. He speaks it with such melody and modulation as he can; "in homely rustic jingle;" but it is his own, and genuine. This is the grand secret for finding readers and retaining them: let him who would move and convince others, be first moved and convinced himself. Horace's rule, *Si vis me flere*,[1] is applicable in a wider sense than the literal one. To every poet, to every writer, we might say: Be true, if you would be believed. Let a man but speak forth with genuine earnestness the thought, the emotion, the actual condition of his own heart; and other men, so strangely are we all knit together by the tie of sympathy, must and will give heed to him. In culture, in extent of view, we may stand above the speaker, or below him; but in either case, his words, if they are earnest and sincere, will find some response within us; for in spite of all casual varieties in outward rank or inward, as face answers to face, so does the heart of man to man.

This may appear a very simple principle, and one which Burns had little merit in discovering. True, the discovery is easy enough: but the practical appliance is not easy; is indeed the fundamental difficulty which all poets have to strive with, and which scarcely one in the hundred ever fairly surmounts. A head too dull to discriminate the true from the false; a heart too dull to love the one at all risks, and to hate the other in spite of all temptations, are alike fatal to a writer. With either, or as more commonly happens, with both of these deficiencies combine a love of distinction, a wish to be original, which is seldom wanting, and we have Affectation, the bane of literature, as Cant, its elder brother, is of morals. How often does the one and the other front us, in poetry, as in life! Great poets themselves are not always free of this vice; nay, it is precisely on a certain sort and degree of greatness that it is most commonly ingrafted. A strong effort after excellence will sometimes solace itself with a mere shadow of success; he who has much to unfold, will sometimes unfold it imperfectly. Byron,[1] for instance, was no common man: yet if we examine his poetry with this view, we shall find it far enough from faultless. Generally speaking, we should say that it is not true. He refreshes us, not with the divine fountain, but too often with vulgar strong waters, stimulating indeed to the taste, but soon ending in dislike, or even nausea. Are his Harolds and Giaours, we would ask, real men; we mean, poetically consistent and conceivable men? Do not these characters, does not the character of their author, which more or less shines through them all, rather appear a thing put on for the occasion; no natural or possible mode of being, but something intended to look much grander than nature? Surely, all these stormful agonies, this volcanic heroism, superhuman contempt and moody desperation, with so much scowling, and teeth-gnashing, and other sulphurous humor, is more like the brawling of a player in some paltry tragedy, which is to last three hours, than the bearing of a man in the business of life, which is to last threescore and ten years. To our minds there is a taint of this sort, something which we should call theatrical, false, affected,[1] in every one of these otherwise so powerful pieces. Perhaps *Don Juan*, especially the latter parts of it, is the only thing approaching to a *sincere* work, he ever wrote; the only work where he showed himself, in any measure, as he was; and seemed so intent on his subject as, for moments, to forget himself. Yet Byron hated this vice; we believe, heartily detested it: nay he had declared formal war against it in words. So difficult is it even for the strongest to make this primary attainment, which might seem the simplest of all: to *read its own consciousness without mistakes*, without errors involuntary or willful! We recollect no poet of Burns's susceptibility who comes before us from the first, and abides with us to the last, with such a total want of affectation. He is an honest man, and an honest writer. In his successes and his failures, in his greatness and his littleness, he is ever clear, simple, true, and glitters with no lustre but his own. We reckon this to be a great virtue; to be, in fact, the root of most other virtues, literary as well as moral.

Here, however, let us say, it is to the Poetry of Burns that we now allude; to those writings which he had time to meditate, and where no special reason existed to warp his critical feeling, or obstruct his endeavor to fulfill it. Certain of his Letters, and other fractions of prose composition, by no means deserve this praise. Here, doubtless, there is not the same natural truth of style; but on the contrary, something not only stiff, but strained and twisted; a certain high-flown inflated tone; the stilting emphasis of which contrasts ill with the firmness and rugged simplicity of even his poorest verses. Thus no man, it would appear, is altogether unaffected. Does not Shakspeare himself sometimes premeditate the sheerest bombast! But even with regard to these Letters of Burns, it is but fair to state that he had two excuses. The first was his comparative deficiency in language. Burns, though for most part he writes with singular force and even gracefulness, is not master of English prose, as he is of Scottish verse; not master of it, we mean, in proportion to the depth and vehemence of his matter. These Letters strike us as the effort of a man to express something which he has no organ fit for expressing. But a second and weightier excuse is to be found in the peculiarity of Burns's social rank. His correspondents are often men whose relation to him he has never accurately ascertained; whom therefore he is either forearming himself against, or else unconsciously flattering, by adopting the style he thinks will please them. At all events we should remember that these faults, even in his Letters, are not the rule, but the exception. Whenever he writes, as one would ever wish to do, to trusted friends and on real interests, his style becomes simple, vigorous, expressive, sometimes even beautiful. His letters to Mrs. Dunlop [1] are uniformly excellent.

But we return to his Poetry. In addition to its Sincerity, it has another peculiar merit, which indeed is but a mode, or perhaps a means, of the foregoing: this displays itself in his choice of subjects; or rather in his indifference as to subjects, and the power he has of making all subjects interesting. The ordinary poet, like the ordinary man, is forever seeking in external circumstances the help which can be found only in himself. In what is familiar and near at hand, he discerns no form or comeliness: home is not poetical but prosaic; it is in some past, distant, conventional heroic world, that poetry resides; were he there and not here, were he thus and not so, it would be well with him. Hence our innumerable host of rose-colored Novels and iron-mailed Epics,[2] with their locality not on the Earth, but somewhere nearer to the Moon. Hence our Virgins of the Sun, and our Knights of the

Cross, malicious Saracens in turbans, and coppercolored Chiefs in wampum, and so many other truculent figures from the heroic times or the heroic climates, who on all hands swarm in our poetry. Peace be with them! But yet, as a great moralist proposed preaching to the men of this century, so would we fain preach to the poets, "a sermon on the duty of staying at home." Let them be sure that heroic ages and heroic climates can do little for them. That form of life has attraction for us, less because it is better or nobler than our own, than simply because it is different; and even this attraction must be of the most transient sort. For will not our own age, one day, be an ancient one; and have as quaint a costume as the rest; not contrasted with the rest, therefore, but ranked along with them, in respect of quaintness? Does Homer interest us now, because he wrote of what passed beyond his native Greece, and two centuries before he was born; or because he wrote what passed in God's world, and in the heart of man, which is the same after thirty centuries? Let our poets look to this: is their feeling really finer, truer, and their vision deeper than that of other men,—they have nothing to fear, even from the humblest subject; is it not so,—they have nothing to hope, but an ephemeral favor, even from the highest.

The poet, we imagine, can never have far to seek for a subject: the elements of his art are in him, and around him on every hand; for him the Ideal world is not remote from the Actual, but under it and within it: nay, he is a poet, precisely because he can discern it there. Wherever there is a sky above him, and a world around him, the poet is in his place; for here too is man's existence, with its infinite longings and small acquirings; its ever-thwarted, ever-renewed endeavors; its unspeakable aspirations, its fears and hopes that wander through Eternity; and all the mystery of brightness and of gloom that it was ever made of, in any age or climate, since man first began to live. Is there not the fifth act[1] of a Tragedy in every death-bed, though it were a peasant's, and a bed of heath? And are wooings and weddings obsolete, that there can be Comedy no longer? Or are men suddenly grown wise, that Laughter must no longer shake his sides, but be cheated of his Farce? Man's life and nature is, as it was, and as it will ever be. But the poet must have an eye to read these things, and a heart to understand them; or they come and pass away before him in vain. He is a *vates*,[2] a seer; a gift of vision has been given him. Has life no meanings for him, which another cannot equally decipher; then he is no poet, and Delphi[3] itself will not make him one.

In this respect, Burns, though not perhaps absolutely a great poet, better manifests his capability, better proves the truth of his genius, than if he had by his own strength kept the whole Minerva Press[4] going, to the end of his literary course. He shows himself at least a poet of Nature's own making; and Nature, after all, is still the grand agent in making poets. We often hear of this and the other external condition being requisite for the existence of a poet. Sometimes it is a certain sort of training; he must have studied certain things, studied for instance "the elder dramatists," and so learned a poetic language; as if poetry lay in the tongue, not in the heart. At other times we are told he must be bred in a certain rank, and must be on a confidential footing with the higher classes; because, above all things, he must see the world. As to seeing the world, we apprehend this will cause him little difficulty, if he have but eyesight to see it with. Without eyesight, indeed, the task might be hard. The blind or the purblind man "travels from Dan to Beersheba[1] and finds it all barren." But happily every poet is born *in* the world; and sees it, with or against his will, every day and every hour he lives. The mysterious workmanship of man's heart, the true light and the inscrutable darkness of man's destiny, reveal themselves not only in capital cities and crowded saloons, but in every hut and hamlet where men have their abode. Nay, do not the elements of all human virtues and all human vices; the passions at once of a Borgia[2] and of a Luther,[3] lie written, in stronger or fainter lines, in the consciousness of every individual bosom, that has practised honest self-examination? Truly, this same world may be seen in Mossgiel[4] and Tarbolton, if we look well, as clearly as it ever came to light in Crockford's,[5] or the Tuileries itself.

But sometimes still harder requisitions are laid on

the poor aspirant to poetry; for it is hinted that he should have *been born* two centuries ago; inasmuch as poetry, about that date, vanished from the earth, and became no longer attainable by men! Such cobweb speculations [1] have, now and then, overhung the field of literature; but they obstruct not the growth of any plant there: the Shakspeare or the Burns, unconsciously and merely as he walks onward, silently brushes them away. Is not every genius an impossibility till he appear? Why do we call him new and original, if *we* saw where his marble was lying, and what fabric he could rear from it? It is not the material but the workman that is wanting. It is not the dark *place* that hinders, but the dim *eye*. A Scottish peasant's life was the meanest and rudest of all lives, till Burns became a poet in it, and a poet of it; found it a *man's* life, and therefore significant to men. A thousand battlefields remain unsung; but the *Wounded Hare* has not perished without its memorial; a balm of mercy yet breathes on us from its dumb agonies, because a poet was there. Our *Hallowe'en* had passed and repassed, in rude awe and laughter, since the era of the Druids; [2] but no Theocritus, [3] till Burns, discerned in it the materials of a Scottish Idyl: neither was the *Holy Fair* [4] any *Council of Trent* [5] or Roman *Jubilee;* [6] but nevertheless, *Superstition* and *Hypocrisy* and *Fun* having been propitious to him, in this man's hand it became a poem, instinct with satire and genuine comic life. Let but the true poet be given us, we repeat it, place him where and how you will, and true poetry will not be wanting. Independently of the essential gift of poetic feeling, as we have now attempted to describe it, a certain rugged sterling worth pervades whatever Burns has written; a virtue, as of green fields and mountain breezes, dwells in his poetry; it is redolent of natural life and hardy natural men. There is a decisive strength in him, and yet a sweet native gracefulness: he is tender, he is vehement, yet without constraint or too visible effort; he melts the heart, or inflames it, with a power which seems habitual and familiar to him. We see that in this man there was the gentleness, the trembling pity of a woman, with the deep earnestness, the force and passionate ardor of a hero. Tears lie in him, and consuming fire; as lightning lurks in the drops of the summer cloud. He has a resonance in his bosom for every note of human feeling; the high and the low, the sad, the ludicrous, the joyful, are welcome in their turns to his "lightly-moved and all-conceiving spirit." And observe with what a fierce prompt force he grasps his subject, be it what it may! How he fixes, as it were, the full image of the matter in his eye; full and clear in every lineament; and catches the real type and essence of it, amid a thousand accidents and superficial circumstances, no one of which misleads him! Is it of reason; some truth to be discovered? No sophistry, no vain surface-logic detains him; quick, resolute, unerring, he pierces through into the marrow of the question; and speaks his verdict with an emphasis that cannot be forgotten. Is it of description; some visual object to be represented? No poet of any age or nation is more graphic than Burns: the characteristic features disclose themselves to him at a glance; three lines from his hand, and we have a likeness. And, in that rough dialect, in that rude, often awkward meter, so clear and definite a likeness! It seems a draughtsman working with a burnt stick; and yet the burin[1] of a Retzsch is not more expressive or exact.

Of this last excellence, the plainest and most comprehensive of all, being indeed the root and foundation of *every* sort of talent, poetical or intellectual, we could produce innumerable instances from the writings of Burns. Take these glimpses of a snowstorm from his *Winter Night* (the italics are ours):

> When biting Boreas,[2] fell and doure,
> *Sharp shivers* thro' the leafless bow'r,
> And Phœbus *gies a short-liv'd glowr*
>   *Far south the lift*,
> *Dim dark'ning thro' the flaky show'r*
>   *Or whirling drift*:
>
> 'Ae night the storm the steeples rock'd
> Poor labor sweet in sleep was lock'd,
> While burns, *wi' snawy wreeths upchok'd*,
>   *Wild-eddying swirl*,
> Or thro' the mining outlet bock'd
>   Down headlong hurl.

Are there not "descriptive touches" here? The describer *saw* this thing; the essential feature and true likeness of every circumstance in it; saw, and not with the eye only. "Poor labor locked in sweet sleep;" the dead stillness of man, unconscious, vanquished, yet not unprotected, while such strife of the material elements rages, and seems to reign supreme in loneliness: this is of the heart as well as of the eye! —Look also at his image of a thaw, and prophesied fall of the *Auld Brig*.[1]

> When heavy, dark, continued, a'-day rains
> Wi' deepening deluges o'erflow the plains;
> When from the hills where springs the brawling Coil,
> Or stately Lugar's *mossy* fountains *boil*,
> Or where the Greenock winds his *moorland* course,
> Or haunted Garpal draws his feeble source,
> Arous'd by blust'ring winds and *spotting* thowes,[2]
> *In mony a torrent down his snaw-broo rowes;*
> *While crashing ice, borne on the roaring spate,*
> *Sweeps dams and mills and brigs a' to the gate;*
> And from Glenbuck down to the Rattonkey,
> Auld Ayr is just one lengthen'd *tumbling* sea;
> Then down ye'll hurl, Deil nor ye never rise!
> And *dash the gumlie jaups up to the pouring skies.*

The last line is in itself a Poussin-picture[3] of that Deluge! The welkin has, as it were, bent down with its weight; the "gumlie jaups" and the "pouring skies" are mingled together; it is a world of rain and ruin.—In respect of mere clearness and minute fidelity, the *Farmer's* commendation of his *Auld Mare*, in plow or in cart, may vie with Homer's Smithy[4] of the Cyclops, or yoking of Priam's Chariot. Nor have we forgotten stout *Burn-the-wind* and his brawny customers, inspired by *Scotch Drink:* but it is needless to multiply examples. One other trait of a much finer sort we select from multitudes of such among his *Songs*. It gives, in a single line, to the saddest feeling the saddest environment and local habitation:

> *The pale Moon is setting beyond the white wave,*
> *And Time is setting wi' me, O;*
> Farewell, false friends! false lover, farewell!
> I'll nae mair trouble them nor thee, O.

This clearness of sight we have called the foundation of all talent; for in fact, unless we *see* our object, how shall we know how to place or prize it, in our understanding, our imagination, our affections? Yet it is not in itself, perhaps, a very high excellence; but capable of being united indifferently with the strongest, or with ordinary power. Homer surpasses all men in this quality: but strangely enough, at no great distance below him are Richardson[1] and Defoe. It belongs, in truth, to what is called a lively mind; and gives no sure indication of the higher endowments that may exist along with it. In all the three cases we have mentioned, it is combined with great garrulity; their descriptions are detailed, ample and lovingly exact; Homer's fire bursts through, from time to time, as if by accident; but Defoe and Richardson have no fire. Burns, again, is not more distinguished by the clearness than by the impetuous force of his conceptions. Of the strength, the piercing emphasis with which he thought, his emphasis of expression may give a humble but the readiest proof. Who ever uttered sharper sayings than his; words more memorable, now by their burning vehemence, now by their cool vigor and laconic pith? A single phrase depicts a whole subject, a whole scene. We hear of "a gentleman that derived his patent of nobility direct from Almighty God." Our Scottish forefathers in the battle-field struggled forward "*red-wat-shod:*"[1] in this one word a full vision of horror and carnage, perhaps too frightfully accurate for Art!

In fact, one of the leading features in the mind of Burns is this vigor of his strictly intellectual perceptions. A resolute force is ever visible in his judgments, and in his feelings and volitions. Professor Stewart[2] says of him, with some surprise: "All the faculties of Burns's mind were, as far as I could judge, equally vigorous; and his predilection for poetry was rather the result of his own enthusiastic and impassioned temper, than of a genius exclusively adapted to that species of composition. From his conversation I should have pronounced him to be fitted to excel in whatever walk of ambition he had chosen to exert his abilities." But this, if we mistake not, is at all times the very essence of a truly poetical endowment. Poetry, except in such cases as that of Keats,[3] where the whole consists in a weak-eyed maudlin sensibility, and a certain vague random tunefulness of nature, is no separate faculty, no organ which can be superadded to the rest, or disjoined from them; but rather the result of their general harmony and completion. The feelings, the gifts that exist in the Poet are those that exist, with more or less development, in every human soul: the imagination, which shudders at the Hell of Dante,[1] is the same faculty, weaker in degree, which called that picture into being. How does the Poet speak to men, with power, but by being still more a man than they? Shakspeare, it has been well observed, in the planning and completing of his tragedies, has shown an Understanding, were it nothing more, which might have governed states, or indited a *Novum Organum*.[2] What Burns's force of understanding may have been, we have less means of judging: it had to dwell among the humblest objects; never saw Philosophy; never rose, except by natural effort and for short intervals, into the region of great ideas. Nevertheless, sufficient indication, if no proof sufficient, remains for us in his works: we discern the brawny movements of a gigantic though untutored strength; and can understand how, in conversation, his quick sure insight into men and things may, as much as aught else about him, have amazed the best thinkers of his time and country.

But, unless we mistake, the intellectual gift of Burns is fine as well as strong. The more delicate relations of things could not well have escaped his eye, for they were intimately present to his heart. The logic of the senate and the forum is indispensable, but not all-sufficient; nay, perhaps the highest Truth is that which will the most certainly elude it. For this logic works by words, and "the highest," it has been said, "cannot be expressed in words." We are not without tokens of an openness for this higher truth also, of a keen though uncultivated sense for it, having existed in Burns. Mr. Stewart, it will be remembered, "wonders," in the passage[1] above quoted, that Burns had formed some distinct conception of the "doctrine of association." We rather think that far subtler things than the doctrine of association had from of old been familiar to him. Here for instance:

"We know nothing," thus writes he, "or next to nothing, of the structure of our souls, so we cannot account for those seeming caprices in them, that one should be particularly pleased with this thing, or struck with that, which, on minds of a different cast, makes no extraordinary impression. I have some favorite flowers in spring, among which are the mountain-daisy, the harebell, the foxglove, the wild-brier rose, the budding birch, and the hoary hawthorn, that I view and hang over with particular delight. I never hear the loud solitary whistle of the curlew in a summer noon, or the wild mixing cadence of a troop of gray plover in an autumnal morning, without feeling an elevation of soul like the enthusiasm of devotion or poetry. Tell me, my dear friend, to what can this be owing? Are we a piece of machinery, which, like the Æolian harp, passive, takes the impression of the passing accident; or do these workings argue something within us above the trodden clod? I own myself partial to such proofs of those awful and important realities: a God that made all things, man's immaterial and immortal nature, and a world of weal or woe beyond death and the grave.''

Force and fineness of understanding are often spoken of as something different from general force and fineness of nature, as something partly independent of them. The necessities of language so require it; but in truth these qualities are not distinct and independent: except in special cases, and from special causes, they ever go together. A man of strong understanding is generally a man of strong character; neither is delicacy in the one kind often divided from delicacy in the other. No one, at all events, is ignorant that in the Poetry of Burns keenness of insight keeps pace with keenness of feeling; that his *light* is not more pervading than his *warmth*. He is a man of the most impassioned temper; with passions not strong only, but noble, and of the sort in which great virtues and great poems take their rise. It is reverence, it is love towards all Nature that inspires him, that opens his eyes to its beauty, and makes heart and voice eloquent in its praise. There is a true old saying, that ''Love furthers knowledge:'' but above all, it is the living essence of that knowledge which makes poets; the first principle of its existence, increase, activity. Of Burns's fervid affection, his generous all-embracing Love, we have spoken already, as of the grand distinction of his nature, seen equally in word and deed, in his Life and in his Writings. It were easy to multiply examples. Not man only, but all that environs man in the material and moral universe, is lovely in his sight: "the hoary hawthorn," the "troop of gray plover," the "solitary curlew," all are dear to him; all live in this Earth along with him, and to all he is knit as in mysterious brotherhood. How touching is it, for instance, that, amidst the gloom of personal misery, brooding over the wintry desolation without him and within him, he thinks of the "ourie cattle" and "silly sheep," and their sufferings in the pitiless storm!

>   I thought me on the ourie cattle,[1]
>   Or silly sheep, wha bide this brattle
>   O' wintry war,
>   Or thro' the drift, deep-lairing, sprattle,
>   Beneath a scaur.
>   Ilk happing bird, wee helpless thing,
>   That in the merry months o' spring
>   Delighted me to hear thee sing,
>   What comes o' thee?
>   Where wilt thou cow'r thy chittering wing,
>   And close thy e'e?

The tenant of the mean hut, with its "ragged roof and chinky wall," has a heart to pity even these! This is worth several homilies on Mercy; for it is the voice of Mercy herself. Burns, indeed, lives in sympathy; his soul rushes forth into all realms of being; nothing that has existence can be indifferent to him. The very Devil he cannot hate with right orthodoxy:

>   But fare you weel, auld Nickie-ben;
>   O, wad[2] ye tak a thought and men'!

> Ye aiblins might,—I dinna ken,—
> Still hae a stake;
> I'm wae to think upo' yon den,
> Even for your sake!

"*He* is the father of curses and lies," said Dr. Slop; "and is cursed and damned already."—"I am sorry for it," quoth my uncle Toby![1]—a Poet without Love were a physical and metaphysical impossibility.

But has it not been said, in contradiction to this principle, that "Indignation makes verses"?[2] It had been so said, and is true enough: but the contradiction is apparent, not real. The Indignation which makes verses is, properly speaking, an inverted Love; the love of some right, some worth, some goodness, belonging to ourselves or others, which has been injured, and which this tempestuous feeling issues forth to defend and avenge. No selfish fury of heart, existing there as a primary feeling, and without its opposite, ever produced much Poetry: otherwise, we suppose, the Tiger were the most musical of all our choristers. Johnson[3] said, he loved a good hater; by which he must have meant, not so much one that hated violently, as one that hated wisely; hated baseness from love of nobleness. However, in spite of Johnson's paradox, tolerable enough for once in speech, but which need not have been so often adopted in print since then, we rather believe that good men deal sparingly in hatred, either wise or unwise: nay that a "good" hater is still a desideratum in this world. The Devil, at least, who passes for the chief and best of that class, is said to be nowise an amiable character.

Of the verses which Indignation makes, Burns has also given us specimens: and among the best that were ever given. Who will forget his "*Dweller*[1] *in yon Dungeon dark;*" a piece that might have been chanted by the Furies of Æschylus?[2] The secrets of the infernal Pit are laid bare; a boundless baleful "darkness visible;"[3] and streaks of hell-fire quivering madly in its black haggard bosom!

> Dweller in yon Dungeon dark,
> Hangman of Creation, mark!
> Who in widow's weeds appears,
> Laden with unhonored years,
> Noosing with care a bursting purse,
> Baited with many a deadly curse!

Why should we speak of *Scots wha hae wi' Wallace bled;* since all know of it, from the king to the meanest of his subjects? This dithyrambic was composed on horseback; in riding in the middle of tempests, over the wildest Galloway moor, in company with a Mr. Syme, who, observing the poet's looks, forbore to speak, —judiciously enough, for a man composing *Bruce's Address* might be unsafe to trifle with. Doubtless this stern hymn was singing itself, as he formed it, through the soul of Burns: but to the external ear, it should be sung with the throat of the whirlwind. So long as there is warm blood in the heart of Scotchman or man, it will move in fierce thrills under this war-ode; the best, we believe, that was ever written by any pen.

Another wild stormful Song, that dwells in our ear and mind with a strange tenacity, is *Macpherson's Farewell*.[1] Perhaps there is something in the tradition itself that co-operates. For was not this grim Celt, this shaggy Northland Cacus,[2] that "lived a life of sturt[3] and strife, and died by treacherie,"—was not he too one of the Nimrods[4] and Napoleons of the earth, in the arena of his own remote misty glens, for want of a clearer and wider one? Nay, was there not a touch of grace given him? A fiber of love and softness, of poetry itself, must have lived in his savage heart: for he composed that air the night before his execution; on the wings of that poor melody his better soul would soar away above oblivion, pain and all the ignominy and despair, which, like an avalanche, was hurling him to the abyss! Here, also, as at Thebes,[5] and in Pelop's line, was material Fate[6] matched against man's Free-will; matched in bitterest though obscure duel; and the ethereal soul sank not, even in its blindness, without a cry which has survived it. But who, except Burns, could have given words to such a soul; words that we never listen to without a strange half-barbarous, half-poetic fellow-feeling?

> *Sae rantingly, sae wantonly,*
> *Sae dauntingly gaed he;*
> *He play'd a spring, and danced it round,*
> *Below the gallows-tree.*

Under a lighter disguise, the same principle of Love, which we have recognized as the great characteristic of Burns, and of all true poets, occasionally manifests itself in the shape of Humor. Everywhere, indeed, in his sunny moods, a full buoyant flood of mirth rolls through the mind of Burns; he rises to the high, and stoops to the low, and is brother and playmate to all Nature. We speak not of his bold and often irresistible faculty of caricature; for this is Drollery rather than Humor: but a much tenderer sportfulness dwells in him; and comes forth here and there, in evanescent and beautiful touches; as in his *Address to the Mouse*, or the *Farmer's Mare*, or in his *Elegy on poor Mailie*, which last may be reckoned his happiest effort of this kind. In these pieces there are traits of a Humor as fine as that of Sterne;[1] yet altogether different, original, peculiar,—the Humor of Burns.

Of the tenderness, the playful pathos, and many other kindred qualities of Burns's Poetry, much more might be said; but now, with these poor outlines of a sketch, we must prepare to quit this part of our subject. To speak of his individual Writings, adequately and with any detail, would lead us far beyond our limits. As already hinted, we can look on but few of these pieces as, in strict critical language, deserving the name of Poems: they are rhymed eloquence, rhymed pathos, rhymed sense; yet seldom essentially melodious, aerial, poetical. *Tam o' Shanter* itself, which enjoys so high a favor, does not appear to us at all decisively to come under this last category. It is not so much a poem, as a piece of sparkling rhetoric; the heart and body of the story still lies hard and dead. He has not gone back, much less carried us back, into that dark, earnest, wondering age, when the tradition was believed, and when it took its rise; he does not attempt, by any new-modeling of his supernatural ware, to strike anew that deep mysterious chord of human nature, which once responded to such things; and which lives in us too, and will forever live, though silent now, or vibrating with far other notes, and to far different issues. Our German readers will understand us, when we say, that he is not the Tieck[1] but the Musäus of this tale. Externally it is all green and living; yet look closer, it is no firm growth, but only ivy on a rock. The piece does not properly cohere: the strange chasm which yawns in our incredulous imaginations between the Ayr public house and the gate of Tophet,[2] is nowhere bridged over, nay the idea of such a bridge is laughed at; and thus the Tragedy of the adventure becomes a mere drunken phantasmagoria, or many-colored spectrum painted on ale-vapors, and the Farce alone has any reality. We do not say that Burns should have made much more of this tradition; we rather think that, for strictly poetical purposes, not much *was* to be made of it. Neither are we blind to the deep, varied, genial power displayed in what he has actually accomplished; but we find far more "Shakspearean" qualities, as these of *Tam o' Shanter* have been fondly named, in many of his other pieces; nay we incline to believe that this latter might have been written, all but quite as well, by a man who, in place of genius, had only possessed talent.

Perhaps we may venture to say, that the most strictly poetical of all his "poems" is one which does not appear in Currie's Edition; but has been often printed before and since, under the humble title of *The Jolly Beggars*. The subject truly is among the lowest in Nature; but it only the more shows our Poet's gift in raising it into the domain of Art. To our minds, this piece seems thoroughly compacted; melted together, refined; and poured forth in one flood of true *liquid* harmony. It is light, airy, soft of movement; yet sharp and precise in its details; every face is a portrait: that *raucle carlin*,[1] that *wee Apollo*, that *Son of Mars*, are Scottish, yet ideal; the scene is at once a dream, and the very Ragcastle of "Poosie Nansie." Farther, it seems in a considerable degree complete, a real self-supporting Whole, which is the highest merit in a poem. The blanket of the Night is drawn asunder for a moment; in full, ruddy, flaming light, these rough tatterdemalions are seen in their boisterous revel; for the strong pulse of Life vindicates its right to gladness even here; and when the curtain closes, we prolong the action, without effort; the next day as the last, our *Caird* and our *Balladmonger* are singing and soldiering; their "brats and callets" are hawking, begging, cheating; and some other night, in new combinations, they will wring from Fate another hour of wassail and good cheer. Apart from the universal sympathy with man which this again bespeaks in Burns, a genuine inspiration and no inconsiderable technical talent are mani-

fested here. There is the fidelity, humor, warm life
and accurate painting and grouping of some Teniers,[1]
for whom hostlers and carousing peasants are not
without significance. It would be strange, doubtless,
to call this the best of Burns's writings: we mean to
say only, that it seems to us the most perfect of its
kind, as a piece of poetical composition, strictly so
called. In the *Beggars' Opera*,[2] in the *Beggars'
Bush*, as other critics have already remarked, there
is nothing which, in real poetic vigor, equals this
Cantata;[3] nothing, as we think, which comes within
many degrees of it.

But by far the most finished, complete and truly
inspired pieces of Burns are, without dispute, to be
found among his *Songs*. It is here that, although
through a small aperture, his light shines with least
obstruction; in its highest beauty and pure sunny
clearness. The reason may be, that Song is a brief
simple species of composition; and requires nothing so
much for its perfection as genuine poetic feeling,
genuine music of heart. Yet the Song has its rules
equally with the Tragedy; rules which in most cases
are poorly fulfilled, in many cases are not so much as
felt. We might write a long essay on the Songs of
Burns; which we reckon by far the best that Britain
has yet produced: for indeed, since the era of Queen
Elizabeth, we know not that, by any other hand,
aught truly worth attention has been accomplished in
this department. True, we have songs enough "by

persons of quality;" we have tawdry, hollow, winebred madrigals; many a rhymed speech "in the flowing and watery vein of Osorius[1] the Portugal Bishop," rich in sonorous words, and, for moral, dashed perhaps with some tint of a sentimental sensuality; all which many persons cease not from endeavoring to sing; though for most part, we fear, the music is but from the throat outwards, or at best from some region far enough short of the *Soul;* not in which, but in a certain inane Limbo[2] of the Fancy, or even in some vaporous debatable land[3] on the outskirts of the Nervous System, most of such madrigals and rhymed speeches seem to have originated.

With the Songs of Burns we must not name these things. Independently of the clear, manly, heartfelt sentiment that ever pervades *his* poetry, his Songs are honest in another point of view: in form, as well as in spirit. They do not *affect* to be set to music, but they actually and in themselves are music; they have received their life, and fashioned themselves together, in the medium of Harmony, as Venus rose[4] from the bosom of the sea. The story, the feeling, is not detailed, but suggested; not *said*, or spouted, in rhetorical completeness and coherence; but *sung*, in fitful gushes, in glowing hints, in fantastic breaks, in *warblings* not of the voice only, but of the whole mind. We consider this to be the essence of a song; and that no songs since the little careless catches, and as it were drops of song, which Shakspeare has here and there sprinkled over his Plays, fulfill this condition in nearly the same degree as most of Burns's do. Such grace and truth of external movement, too, presupposes in general a corresponding force and truth of sentiment and inward meaning. The Songs of Burns are not more perfect in the former quality than in the latter. With what tenderness he sings, yet with what vehemence and entireness! There is a piercing wail in his sorrow, the purest rapture in his joy; he burns with the sternest ire, or laughs with the loudest or sliest mirth; and yet he is sweet and soft, "sweet as the smile when fond lovers meet, and soft as their parting tear." If we farther take into account the immense variety of his subjects; how, from the loud flowing revel in *Willie brew'd a Peck o' Maut*, to the still, rapt enthusiasm of sadness for *Mary in Heaven;* from the glad kind greeting of *Auld Lang Syne*, or the comic archness of *Duncan Gray*, to the fire-eyed fury of *Scots wha hae wi' Wallace bled*, he has found a tone and words for every mood of man's heart,—it will seem a small praise if we rank him as the first of all our Song-writers; for we know not where to find one worthy of being second to him.

It is on his Songs, as we believe, that Burns's chief influence as an author will ultimately be found to depend: nor, if our Fletcher's aphorism [1] is true, shall we account this a small influence. "Let me make the songs of a people," said he, "and you shall make its laws." Surely, if ever any Poet might have equaled himself with Legislators on this ground, it was Burns.

His Songs are already part of the mother-tongue, not of Scotland only but of Britain, and of the millions that in all ends of the earth speak a British language. In hut and hall, as the heart unfolds itself in many-colored joy and woe of existence, the *name*, the *voice* of that joy and that woe, is the name and voice which Burns has given them. Strictly speaking, perhaps no British man has so deeply affected the thoughts and feelings of so many men, as this solitary and altogether private individual, with means apparently the humblest.

In another point of view, moveover, we incline to think that Burns's influence may have been considerable: we mean, as exerted specially on the Literature of his country, at least on the Literature of Scotland. Among the great changes which British, particularly Scottish literature, has undergone since that period, one of the greatest will be found to consist in its remarkable increase of nationality. Even the English writers, most popular in Burns's time, were little distinguished for their literary patriotism, in this its best sense. A certain attenuated cosmopolitanism had, in good measure, taken place of the old insular home-feeling; literature was, as it were, without any local environment; was not nourished by the affections which spring from a native soil. Our Grays and Glovers [1] seemed to write almost as if *in vacuo*;[2] the thing written bears no mark of place; it is not written so much for Englishmen, as for men; or rather, which is the inevitable result of this, for certain Generalizations which philosophy termed men. Goldsmith [1] is an exception: not so Johnson; the scene of his *Rambler* [2] is little more English than that of his *Rasselas.*

But if such was, in some degree, the case with England, it was, in the highest degree, the case with Scotland. In fact, our Scottish literature had, at that period, a very singular aspect; unexampled, so far as we know, except perhaps at Geneva, where the same state of matters appears still to continue. For a long period after Scotland became British, we had no literature: at the date when Addison and Steele [3] were writing their *Spectators,* our good Thomas Boston [4] was writing, with the noblest intent, but alike in defiance of grammar and philosophy, his *Fourfold State of Man.* Then came the schisms in our National Church, and the fiercer schisms in our Body Politic: Theologic ink, and Jacobite blood,[5] with gall enough in both cases, seemed to have blotted out the intellect of the country: however, it was only obscured, not obliterated. Lord Kames [6] made nearly the first attempt at writing English; and ere long, Hume,[7] Robertson, Smith, and a whole host of followers, attracted hither the eyes of all Europe. And yet in this brilliant resuscitation of our "fervid genius," there was nothing truly Scottish, nothing indigenous; except, perhaps, the natural impetuosity of intellect, which we sometimes claim and are sometimes upbraided with, as a characteristic of our nation. It is curious to remark that Scotland, so full of writers, had no Scottish culture, nor indeed any English; our culture was almost exclusively French. It was by studying Racine [1] and Voltaire,[2] Batteux [3] and Boileau,[4] that Kames had trained himself to be a critic and philosopher; it was the light of Montesquieu [5] and Mably [6] that guided Robertson in his political speculations; Quesnay's [7] lamp that kindled the lamp of Adam Smith. Hume was too rich a man to borrow; and perhaps he reacted on the French more than he was acted on by them: but neither had he aught to do with Scotland; Edinburgh, equally with La Flèche,[8] was but the lodging and laboratory, in which he not so much morally *lived*, as metaphysically *investigated*. Never, perhaps, was there a class of writers so clear and well ordered, yet so totally destitute, to all appearance, of any patriotic affection, nay of any human affection whatever. The French wits of the period were as unpatriotic: but their general deficiency in moral principles, not to say their avowed sensuality and unbelief in all virtue, strictly so called, render this accountable enough. We hope, there is a patriotism founded on something better than prejudice; that our country may be dear to us, without injury to our philosophy; that in loving and justly prizing all other lands, we may prize justly, and yet love before all others, our own stern Motherland, and the venerable Structure of social and moral Life, which Mind has through long ages been building up for us there. Surely there is nourishment for the better part of man's heart in all this: surely the roots, that have fixed themselves in the very core of man's being, may be so cultivated as to grow up not into briers, but into roses, in the field of his life! Our Scottish sages have no such propensities: the field of their life shows neither briers nor roses; but only a flat, continuous thrashing-floor for Logic, whereon all questions, from the "Doctrine[1] of Rent" to the "Natural History of Religion," are thrashed and sifted with the same mechanical impartiality!

With Sir Walter Scott at the head of our literature, it cannot be denied that much of this evil is past, or rapidly passing away: our chief literary men, whatever other faults they may have, no longer live among us like a French Colony, or some knot of Propaganda[2] Missionaries; but like natural-born subjects of the soil, partaking and sympathizing in all our attachments, humors and habits. Our literature no longer grows in water but in mould, and with the true racy virtues of the soil and climate. How much of this change may be due to Burns, or to any other individual, it might be difficult to estimate. Direct literary imitation of Burns was not to be looked for. But his example, in the fearless adoption of domestic subjects, could not but operate from afar; and certainly in no heart did the love of country ever burn with a warmer glow than in that of Burns: "a tide of Scottish prejudice," as he modestly calls this deep and generous feeling, "had been poured along his veins; and he felt that it would boil there till the flood-gates shut in eternal rest." It seemed to him, as if *he* could do so little for his country, and yet would so gladly have done all. One small province stood open for him,— that of Scottish Song; and how eagerly he entered on it, how devotedly he labored there! In his toilsome journeyings, this object never quits him; it is the little happy-valley of his careworn heart. In the gloom of his own affliction, he eagerly searches after some lonely brother of the muse, and rejoices to snatch one other name from the oblivion that was covering it! These were early feelings, and they abode with him to the end:

> . . . A wish (I mind its power),
> A wish, that to my latest hour
> Will strongly heave my breast,—
> That I, for poor auld Scotland's sake,
> Some useful plan or book could make,
> Or sing a sang at least.
>
> The rough bur Thistle spreading wide
>   Among the bearded bear,
> I turn'd my weeding-clips aside,
>   And spared the symbol dear.[1]

But to leave the mere literary character of Burns, which has already detained us too long. Far more interesting than any of his written works, as it appears to us, are his acted ones: the Life he willed and was fated to lead among his fellow-men. These Poems are but like little rhymed fragments scattered here and there in the grand unrhymed Romance of his earthly existence; and it is only when intercalated[2] in this at their proper places, that they attain their full measure of significance. And this, too, alas, was but a fragment! The plan of a mighty edifice had been sketched; some columns, porticos, firm masses of building, stand completed; the rest more or less clearly indicated; with many a far-stretching tendency, which only studious and friendly eyes can now trace towards the purposed termination. For the work is broken off in the middle, almost in the beginning; and rises among us, beautiful and sad, at once unfinished and a ruin! If charitable judgment was necessary in estimating his Poems, and justice required that the aim and the manifest power to fulfill it must often be accepted for the fulfillment; much more is this the case in regard to his Life, the sum and result of all his endeavors, where his difficulties came upon him not in detail only, but in mass; and so much has been left unaccomplished, nay was mistaken, and altogether marred.

Properly speaking, there is but one era in the life of Burns, and that the earliest. We have not youth and manhood, but only youth: for, to the end, we discern no decisive change in the complexion of his character; in his thirty-seventh year he is still, as it were, in youth. With all that resoluteness of judgment, that penetrating insight, and singular maturity of intellectual power, exhibited in his writings, he never attains to any clearness regarding himself; to the last, he never ascertains his peculiar aim, even with such distinctness as is common among ordinary men; and therefore never can pursue it with that singleness of will, which insures success and some contentment to such men. To the last, he wavers between two purposes: glorying in his talent, like a true poet, he yet cannot consent to make this his chief and sole glory, and to follow it as the one thing needful, through poverty or riches, through good or evil report. Another far meaner ambition still cleaves to him; he must dream and struggle about a certain "Rock[1] of Independence;" which, natural and even admirable as it might be, was still but a warring with the world, on the comparatively insignificant ground of his being more completely or less completely supplied with money than others; of his standing at a higher or a lower altitude in general estimation than others. For the world still appears to him, as to the young, in borrowed colors: he expects from it what it cannot give to any man; seeks for contentment, not within himself, in action and wise effort, but from without, in the kindness of circumstances, in love, friendship, honor, pecuniary ease. He would be happy, not actively and in himself, but passively and from some ideal cornucopia of Enjoyments, not earned by his own labor, but showered on him by the beneficence of Destiny. Thus, like a young man, he cannot gird himself up for any worthy well-calculated goal, but swerves to and fro, between passionate hope and remorseful disappointment: rushing onwards with a deep tempestuous force, he surmounts or breaks asunder many a barrier; travels, nay advances far, but advancing only under uncertain guidance, is ever and anon turned from his path; and to the last cannot reach the only true happiness of a man, that of clear decided Activity in the sphere for which, by nature and circumstances, he has been fitted and appointed.

We do not say these things in dispraise of Burns; nay, perhaps, they but interest us the more in his favor. This blessing is not given soonest to the best; but rather, it is often the greatest minds that are latest in obtaining it; for where most is to be developed, most time may be required to develop it. A complex condition had been assigned him from without; as complex a condition from within: no "preëstablished harmony" existed between the clay soil of Mossgiel and the empyrean soul of Robert Burns; it was not wonderful that the adjustment between them should have been long postponed, and his arm long cumbered, and his sight confused, in so vast and discordant an economy as he had been appointed steward over. Byron was, at his death, but a year younger than Burns; and through life, as it might have appeared, far more simply situated: yet in him too we can trace no such adjustment, no such moral manhood; but at best, and only a little before his end, the beginning of what seemed such.

By much the most striking incident in Burns's Life is his journey to Edinburgh; but perhaps a still more important one is his residence at Irvine, so early as in his twenty-third year. Hitherto his life had been poor and toilworn; but otherwise not ungenial, and, with all its distresses, by no means unhappy. In his parentage, deducting outward circumstances, he had every reason to reckon himself fortunate. His father was a man of thoughtful, intense, earnest character, as the best of our peasants are; valuing knowledge, possessing some, and, what is far better and rarer, open-minded for more: a man with a keen insight and devout heart; reverent towards God, friendly therefore at once, and fearless towards all that God has made: in one word, though but a hard-handed peasant, a complete and fully unfolded *Man*. Such a father is seldom found in any rank in society; and was worth descending far in society to seek. Unfortunately, he was very poor; had he been even a little richer, almost never so little, the whole might have issued far otherwise. Mighty events turn on a straw; the crossing of a brook[1] decides the conquest of the world. Had this William Burns's small seven acres of nursery-ground anywise prospered, the boy Robert had been sent to school; had struggled forward, as so many weaker men do, to some university; come forth not as a rustic wonder, but as a regular well-trained intellectual workman, and changed the whole course of British Literature,—for it lay in him to have done this! But the nursery did not prosper; poverty sank his whole family below the help of even our cheap school-system: Burns remained a hard-worked plowboy, and British Literature took its own course. Nevertheless, even in this rugged scene there is much to nourish him. If he drudges, it is with his brother, and for his father and mother, whom he loves, and would fain shield from want. Wisdom is not banished from their poor hearth, nor the balm of natural feeling: the solemn words, *Let us worship God*, are heard there from a "priest-like father;"[1] if threatenings of unjust men throw mother and children into tears, these are tears not of grief only, but of holiest affection; every heart in that humble group feels itself the closer knit to every other; in their hard warfare they are there together, a "little band of brethren." Neither are such tears, and the deep beauty that dwells in them, their only portion. Light visits the hearts as it does the eyes of all living: there is a force, too, in this youth, that enables him to trample on misfortune; nay to bind it under his feet to make him sport. For a bold, warm, buoyant humor of character has been given him; and so the thick-coming shapes of evil are welcomed with a gay, friendly irony, and in their closest pressure he bates no jot of heart or hope. Vague yearnings of ambition fail not, as he grows up; dreamy fancies hang like cloud-cities around him; the curtain of Existence is slowly rising, in many-colored splendor and gloom: and the auroral light of first love is gilding his horizon, and the music of song is on his path; and so he walks

. . . . . in glory and in joy,[2]
Behind his plow, upon the mountain side.

We ourselves know, from the best evidence, that up to this date Burns was happy; nay that he was the gayest, brightest, most fantastic, fascinating being to be found in the world; more so even than he ever afterwards appeared. But now, at this early age, he quits the paternal roof; goes forth into looser, louder, more exciting society; and becomes initiated in those dissipations, those vices, which a certain class of philosophers have asserted to be a natural preparative for entering on active life; a kind of mud-bath, in which the youth is, as it were, necessitated to steep, and, we suppose, cleanse himself, before the real toga of Manhood can be laid on him. We shall not dispute much with this class of philosophers; we hope they are mistaken; for Sin and Remorse so easily beset us at all stages of life, and are always such indifferent company, that it seems hard we should, at any stage, be forced and fated not only to meet but to yield to them, and even serve for a term in their leprous armada. We hope it is not so. Clear we are, at all events, it cannot be the training one receives in this Devil's-service, but only our determining to desert from it, that fits us for true manly Action. We become men, not after we have been dissipated, and disappointed in the chase of false pleasure; but after we have ascertained, in any way, what impassable barriers hem us in through this life; how mad it is to hope for contentment to our infinite soul from the *gifts* of this extremely finite world; that a man must be sufficient for himself; and that for suffering and enduring there is no remedy but striving and doing. Manhood begins when we have in any way made truce with Necessity; begins even when we have surrendered to Necessity, as the most part only do; but begins joyfully and hopefully only when we have reconciled ourselves to Necessity; and thus, in reality, triumphed over it, and felt that in Necessity we are free. Surely, such lessons as this last, which in one shape or other, is the grand lesson for every mortal man, are better learned from the lips of a devout mother, in the looks and actions of a devout father, while the heart is yet soft and pliant, than in collision with the sharp adamant of Fate, attracting us to shipwreck us, when the heart is grown hard, and may be broken before it will become contrite. Had Burns continued to learn this, as he was already learning it, in his father's cottage, he would have learned it fully, which he never did; and been saved many a lasting aberration, many a bitter hour and year of remorseful sorrow.

It seems to us another circumstance of fatal import in Burns's history, that at this time too he became involved in the religious quarrels of his district; that he was enlisted and feasted, as the fighting man of the New-Light Priesthood, in their highly unprofitable warfare. At the tables of these free-minded clergy he learned much more than was needful for him. Such liberal ridicule of fanaticism awakened in his mind scruples about Religion itself; and a whole world of Doubts, which it required quite another set of conjurors than these men to exorcise. We do not say that such an intellect as his could have escaped similar doubts at some period of his history; or even that he could, at a later period, have come through them altogether victorious and unharmed: but it seems peculiarly unfortunate that this time, above all others, should have been fixed for the encounter. For now, with principles assailed by evil example from without, by "passions[1] raging like demons" from within, he had little need of skeptical misgivings to whisper treason in the heat of the battle, or to cut off his retreat if he were already defeated. He loses his feeling of innocence; his mind is at variance with itself; the old divinity no longer presides there; but wild Desires and wild Repentance alternately oppress him. Ere long, too, he has committed himself before the world; his character for sobriety, dear to a Scottish peasant as few corrupted worldlings can even conceive, is destroyed in the eyes of men; and his only refuge consists in trying to disbelieve his guiltiness, and is but a refuge of lies. The blackest desperation now gathers over him, broken only by red lightnings of remorse. The whole fabric of his life is blasted asunder; for now not only his character, but his personal liberty, is to be lost; men and Fortune are leagued for his hurt; "hungry[2] Ruin has him in the wind." He sees no escape but the saddest of all: exile from his loved country, to a country in every sense inhospitable and abhorrent to him. While the "gloomy night is gathering fast," in mental storm and solitude, as well as in physical, he sings his wild farewell to Scotland:[3]

> Farewell, my friends; farewell, my foes!
> My peace with these, my love with those:
> The bursting tears my heart declare;
> Adieu, my native banks of Ayr!

Light breaks suddenly in on him in floods; but still a false transitory light, and no real sunshine. He is invited to Edinburgh; hastens thither with anticipating heart; is welcomed as in a triumph, and with universal blandishment and acclamation; whatever is wisest, whatever is greatest or loveliest there, gathers round him, to gaze on his face, to show him honor, sympathy, affection. Burns's appearance among the sages and nobles of Edinburgh must be regarded as one of the most singular phenomena in modern Literature; almost like the appearance of some Napoleon among the crowned sovereigns of modern Politics. For it is nowise as "a mockery[1] king," set there by favor, transiently and for a purpose, that he will let himself be treated; still less is he a mad Rienzi,[2] whose sudden elevation turns his too weak head: but he stands there on his own basis; cool, unastonished, holding his equal rank from Nature herself; putting forth no claim which there is not strength *in* him, as well as about him, to vindicate. Mr. Lockhart has some forcible observations on this point:

"It needs no effort of imagination," says he, "to conceive what the sensations of an isolated set of scholars (almost all either clergymen or professors) must have been in the presence of this big-boned, black-browed, brawny stranger, with his great flashing eyes, who, having forced his way among them from the plow-tail at a single stride, manifested in the whole strain of his bearing and conversation a most thorough conviction, that in the society of the most eminent men of his nation he was exactly where he was entitled to be; hardly deigned to flatter them by exhibiting even an occasional symptom of being flattered by their notice; by turns calmly measured himself against the most cultivated understandings of his time in discussion; overpowered the *bon-mots* of the most celebrated convivialists by broad floods of merriment, impregnated with all the burning life of genius; astounded bosoms habitually enveloped in the thrice-piled folds of social reserve, by compelling them to tremble—nay, to tremble visibly—beneath the fearless touch of natural pathos; and all this without indicating the smallest willingness to be ranked among those professional ministers of excitement, who are content to be paid in money and smiles for doing what the spectators and auditors would be ashamed of doing in their own persons, even if they had the power of doing it; and last, and probably worst of all, who was known to be in the habit of enlivening societies which they would have scorned to approach, still more frequently than their own, with eloquence no less magnificent; with wit, in all likelihood still more daring; often enough, as the superiors whom he fronted without alarm might have guessed from the beginning, and had ere long no occasion to guess, with wit pointed at themselves.''

The farther we remove from this scene, the more singular will it seem to us: details of the exterior aspect of it are already full of interest. Most readers recollect Mr. Walker's personal interviews with Burns as among the best passages of his Narrative: a time will come when this reminiscence of Sir Walter Scott's, slight though it is, will also be precious:

"'As for Burns," writes Sir Walter, "I may truly say, *Virgilium vidi tantum*.[1] I was a lad of fifteen in 1786-7, when he came first to Edinburgh, but had sense and feeling enough to be much interested in his poetry, and would have given the world to know him: but I had very little acquaintance with any literary people, and still less with the gentry of the west country, the two sets that he most frequented. Mr. Thomas Grierson was at that time a clerk of my father's. He knew Burns, and promised to ask him to his lodgings to dinner; but had no opportunity to keep his word; otherwise I might have seen more of this distinguished man. As it was, I saw him one day at the late venerable Professor Ferguson's,[2] where there were several gentlemen of literary reputation, among whom I remember the celebrated Mr. Dugald Stewart. Of course, we youngsters sat silent, looked and listened. The only thing I remember which was remarkable in Burns's manner, was the effect produced upon him by a print of Bunbury's,[3] representing a soldier lying dead on the snow, his dog sitting in misery on one side,—on the other, his widow, with a child in her arms. These lines were written beneath:

  " 'Cold on Canadian hills, or Minden's plain,
    Perhaps that mother wept her soldier slain;

Bent o'er her babe, her eye dissolved in dew,
The big drops mingling with the milk he drew,
Gave the sad presage of his future years,
The child of misery baptized in tears.'

"Burns seemed much affected by the print, or rather by the ideas which it suggested to his mind. He actually shed tears. He asked whose the lines were; and it chanced that nobody but myself remembered that they occur in a half-forgotten poem of Langhorne's [1] called by the unpromising title of "The Justice of Peace." I whispered my information to a friend present; he mentioned it to Burns, who rewarded me with a look and a word, which, though of mere civility, I then received and still recollect with very great pleasure.

"His person was strong and robust; his manners rustic, not clownish; a sort of dignified plainness and simplicity, which received part of its effect perhaps from one's knowledge of his extraordinary talents. His features are represented in Mr. Nasmyth's picture:[2] but to me it conveys the idea that they are diminished, as if seen in perspective. I think his countenance was more massive than it looks in any of the portraits. I should have taken the poet, had I not known what he was, for a very sagacious country farmer of the old Scotch school, *i.e.* none of your modern agriculturists who keep laborers for their drudgery, but the *douce gudeman*[3] who held his own plow. There was a strong expression of sense and shrewdness in all his lineaments; the eye alone, I think, indicated the poetical character and temperament. It was large, and of a dark cast, which glowed (I say literally *glowed*) when he spoke with feeling or interest. I never saw such another eye in a human head, though I have seen the most distinguished men of my time. His conversation expressed perfect self-confidence, without the slightest presumption. Among the men who were the most learned of their time and country, he expressed himself with perfect firmness, but without the least intrusive forwardness; and when he differed in opinion, he did not hesitate to express it firmly, yet at the same time with modesty. I do not remember any part of his conversation distinctly enough to be quoted; nor did I ever see him again, except in the street, where he did not recognize me, as I could not expect he should. He was much caressed in Edinburgh: but (considering what literary emoluments have been since his day) the efforts made for his relief were extremely trifling.

"I remember, on this occasion I mention, I thought Burns's acquaintance with English poetry was rather limited; and also that, having twenty times the abilities of Allan Ramsay and of Fergusson, he talked of them with too much humility as his models: there was doubtless national predilection in his estimate.

"This is all I can tell you about Burns. I have only to add, that his dress corresponded with his manner. He was like a farmer dressed in his best to dine with the laird. I do not speak *in malam partem*,[1] when I say, I never saw a man in company with his superiors in station or information more perfectly free from either the reality or the affectation of embarrassment. I was told, but did not observe it, that his address to females was extremely deferential, and always with a turn either to the pathetic or humorous, which engaged their attention particularly. I have heard the late Duchess of Gordon remark this.—I do not know anything I can add to these recollections of forty years since.''

The conduct of Burns under this dazzling blaze of favor; the calm, unaffected, manly manner in which he not only bore it, but estimated its value, has justly been regarded as the best proof that could be given of his real vigor and integrity of mind. A little natural vanity, some touches of hypocritical modesty, some glimmerings of affectation, at least some fear of being thought affected, we could have pardoned in almost any man; but no such indication is to be traced here. In his unexampled situation the young peasant is not a moment perplexed; so many strange lights do not confuse him, do not lead him astray. Nevertheless, we cannot but perceive that this winter did him great and lasting injury. A somewhat clearer knowledge of men's affairs, scarcely of their characters, it did afford him; but a sharper feeling of Fortune's unequal arrangements in their social destiny it also left with him. He had seen the gay and gorgeous arena, in which the powerful are born to play their parts; nay had himself stood in the midst of it; and he felt more bitterly than ever, that here he was but a looker-on, and had no part or lot in that splendid game. From this time a jealous indignant fear of social degradation takes possession of him; and perverts, so far as aught could pervert, his private contentment, and his feelings towards his richer fellows. It was clear to Burns that he had talent enough to make a fortune, or a hundred fortunes, could he but have rightly willed this; it was clear also that he willed something far different, and therefore could not make one. Unhappy it was that he had not power to choose the one, and reject the other; but must halt forever between two opinions, two objects; making hampered advancement towards either. But so is it with many men: we "long for the merchandise, yet would fain keep the price;" and so stand chaffering with Fate, in vexatious altercation, till the night come, and our fair is over!

The Edinburgh Learned of that period were in general more noted for clearness of head than for warmth of heart: with the exception of the good old Blacklock,[1] whose help was too ineffectual, scarcely one among them seems to have looked at Burns with any true sympathy, or indeed much otherwise than as at a highly curious *thing*. By the great also he is treated in the customary fashion; entertained at their tables and dismissed: certain modica of pudding and praise are, from time to time, gladly exchanged for the fascination of his presence; which exchange once affected, the bargain is finished, and each party goes his several way. At the end of this strange season,

Burns gloomily sums up his gains and losses, and meditates on the chaotic future. In money he is somewhat richer; in fame and the show of happiness, infinitely richer; but in the substance of it, as poor as ever. Nay poorer; for his heart is now maddened still more with the fever of worldly Ambition; and through long years the disease will rack him with unprofitable sufferings, and weaken his strength for all true and nobler aims.

What Burns was next to do or to avoid; how a man so circumstanced was now to guide himself towards his true advantage, might at this point of time have been a question for the wisest. It was a question too, which apparently he was left altogether to answer for himself: of his learned or rich patrons it had not struck any individual to turn a thought on this so trivial matter. Without claiming for Burns the praise of perfect sagacity, we must say, that his Excise and Farm scheme[1] does not seem to us a very unreasonable one; that we should be at a loss, even now, to suggest one decidedly better. Certain of his admirers have felt scandalized at his ever resolving to *gauge;*[2] and would have had him lie at the pool,[3] till the spirit of Patronage[4] stirred the waters, that so, with one friendly plunge, all his sorrows might be healed. Unwise counselors! They know not the manner of this spirit; and how, in the lap of most golden dreams, a man might have happiness, were it not that in the interim he must die of hunger! It reflects credit on the manliness and sound sense of Burns, that he felt so early on what ground he was standing, and preferred self-help, on the humblest scale, to dependence and inaction, though with hope of far more splendid possibilities. But even these possibilities were not rejected in his scheme: he might expect, if it chanced that he *had* any friend, to rise, in no long period, into something even like opulence and leisure; while again, if it chanced that he had no friend, he could still live in security; and for the rest, he "did not intend to borrow honor from any profession." We reckon that his plan was honest and well-calculated: all turned on the execution of it. Doubtless it failed; yet not, we believe, from any vice inherent in itself. Nay, after all, it was no failure of external means, but of internal, that overtook Burns. His was no bankruptcy of the purse, but of the soul; to his last day, he owed no man anything.

Meanwhile he begins well: with two good and wise actions. His donation to his mother, munificent from a man whose income had lately been seven pounds a year, was worthy of him, and not more than worthy. Generous also, and worthy of him, was the treatment of the woman whose life's welfare now depended on his pleasure. A friendly observer might have hoped serene days for him: his mind is on the true road to peace with itself: what clearness he still wants will be given as he proceeds; for the best teacher of duties, that still lie dim to us, is the Practice of those we see and have at hand. Had the "patrons of genius," who could give him nothing, but taken nothing from him, at least nothing more! The wounds of his heart would have healed, vulgar ambition would have died away. Toil and Frugality would have been welcome, since Virtue dwelt with them: and Poetry would have shone through them as of old: and in her clear ethereal light, which was his own by birthright, he might have looked down on his earthly destiny, and all its obstructions, not with patience only, but with love.

But the patrons of genius would not have it so. Picturesque tourists,[1] all manner of fashionable danglers after literature, and, far worse, all manner of convivial Mæcenases,[2] hovered round him in his retreat; and his good as well as his weak qualities secured them influence over him. He was flattered by their notice; and his warm social nature made it impossible for him to shake them off, and hold on his way apart from them. These men, as we believe, were proximately the means of his ruin. Not that they meant him any ill; they only meant themselves a little good; if he suffered harm, let *him* look to it! But they wasted his precious time and his precious talent; they disturbed his composure, broke down his returning habits of temperance and assiduous contented exertion. Their pampering was baneful to him; their cruelty, which soon followed, was equally baneful. The old grudge against Fortune's inequality awoke with new bitterness in their neighborhood; and Burns had no retreat but to "the Rock of Independence," which is but an air-castle after all, that looks well at a distance, but will screen no one from real wind and wet. Flushed with irregular excitement, exasperated alternately by contempt of others, and contempt of himself, Burns was no longer regaining his peace of mind, but fast losing it forever. There was a hollowness at the heart of his life, for his conscience did not now approve what he was doing. Amid the vapors of unwise enjoyment, of bootless remorse, and angry discontent with Fate, his true loadstar, a life of Poetry, with Poverty, nay with Famine if it must be so, was too often altogether hidden from his eyes. And yet he sailed a sea, where without some such loadstar there was no right steering. Meteors of French Politics rise before him, but these were not *his* stars. An accident this, which hastened, but did not originate, his worst distresses. In the mad contentions of that time, he comes in collision[1] with certain official Superiors; is wounded by them; cruelly lacerated, we should say, could a dead mechanical implement, in any case, be called cruel: and shrinks, in indignant pain, into deeper self-seclusion, into gloomier moodiness than ever. His life has now lost its unity: it is a life of fragments; led with little aim, beyond the melancholy one of securing its own continuance,—in fits of wild false joy when such offered, and of black despondency when they passed away. His character before the world begins to suffer: calumny is busy with him; for a miserable man makes more enemies than friends. Some faults he has fallen into, and a thousand misfortunes; but deep criminality is what he stands accused of, and they that are *not* without sin cast the first stone at him![1] For is he not a well-wisher to the French Revolution, a Jacobin,[2] and therefore in that one act guilty of all? These accusations, political and moral, it has since appeared, were false enough: but the world hesitated little to credit them. Nay his convivial Mæcenases themselves were not the last to do it. There is reason to believe that, in his later years, the Dumfries Aristocracy had partly withdrawn themselves from Burns, as from a tainted person, no longer worthy of their acquaintance. That painful class, stationed, in all provincial cities, behind the outmost breastwork of Gentility, there to stand siege and do battle against the intrusions of Grocerdom[3] and Grazierdom, had actually seen dishonor in the society of Burns, and branded him with their veto; had, as we vulgarly say, *cut* him! We find one passage in this Work of Mr. Lockhart's, which will not out of our thoughts:

"A gentleman of that county, whose name I have already more than once had occasion to refer to, has often told me that he was seldom more grieved, than when riding into Dumfries one fine summer evening about this time to attend a county ball, he saw Burns walking alone, on the shady side of the principal street of the town, while the opposite side was gay with successive groups of gentlemen and ladies, all drawn together for the festivities of the night, not one of whom appeared willing to recognize him. The horseman dismounted, and joined Burns, who on his proposing to cross the street said: 'Nay, nay, my young friend, that's all over now;' and quoted, after a pause, some verses of Lady Grizzel Baillie's [1] pathetic ballad:

> " 'His bonnet stood ance fu' fair on his brow,
> His auld ane look'd better than mony ane's new;
> But now he lets 't wear ony way it will hing,
> And casts himsell dowie upon the corn-bing.
>
> O, were we young as we ance hae been,
> We sud hae been gallopping down on yon green,
> And linking it ower the lily-white lea!
> *And werena my heart light, I wad die.*'

It was little in Burns's character to let his feelings on certain subjects escape in this fashion. He, immediately after reciting these verses, assumed the sprightliness of his most pleasing manner; and taking his young friend home with him, entertained him very agreeably till the hour of the ball arrived."

Alas! when we think that Burns now sleeps "where [2] bitter indignation can no longer lacerate his heart," and that most of those fair dames and frizzled gentlemen already lie at his side, where the breastwork of gentility is quite thrown down,—who would not sigh over the thin delusions and foolish toys that divide heart from heart, and make man unmerciful to his brother!

It was not now to be hoped that the genius of Burns would ever reach maturity, or accomplish aught worthy of itself. His spirit was jarred in its melody; not the soft breath of natural feeling, but the rude hand of Fate, was now sweeping over the strings. And yet what harmony was in him, what music even in his discords! How the wild tones had a charm for the simplest and the wisest; and all men felt and knew that here also was one of the Gifted! "If he entered [1] an inn at midnight, after all the inmates were in bed, the news of his arrival circulated from the cellar to the garret; and ere ten minutes had elapsed, the landlord and all his guests were assembled!" Some brief pure moments of poetic life were yet appointed him, in the composition of his Songs. We can understand how he grasped at this employment; and how too, he spurned [2] all other reward for it but what the labor itself brought him. For the soul of Burns, though scathed and marred, was yet living in its full moral strength, though sharply conscious of its errors and abasement: and here, in his destitution and degradation, was one act of seeming nobleness and self-devotedness left even for him to perform. He felt too, that with all the "thoughtless [3] follies" that had "laid him low," the world was unjust and cruel to him; and he silently appealed to another and calmer time. Not as a hired soldier, but as a patriot, would he strive for the glory of his country: so he cast from him the poor sixpence a-day, and served zealously as a volunteer.[4] Let us not grudge him this last luxury of his existence; let him not have appealed to us in vain! The money was not necessary to him; he struggled through without it: long since, these guineas would have been gone, and now the high-mindedness of refusing them will plead for him in all hearts forever.

We are here arrived at the crisis of Burns's life; for matters had now taken such a shape with him as could not long continue. If improvement was not to be looked for, Nature could only for a limited time maintain this dark and maddening warfare against the world and itself. We are not medically informed whether any continuance of years was, at this period, probable for Burns; whether his death is to be looked on as in some sense an accidental event, or only as the natural consequence of the long series of events that had preceded. The latter seems to be the likelier opinion; and yet it is by no means a certain one. At all events, as we have said, *some* change could not be very distant. Three gates of deliverance, it seems to us, were open for Burns: clear poetical activity; madness; or death. The first, with longer life, was still possible, though not probable; for physical causes were beginning to be concerned in it: and yet Burns had an iron resolution; could he but have seen and felt, that not only his highest glory, but his first duty, and the true medicine for all his woes, lay here. The second was still less probable; for his mind was ever among the clearest and firmest. So the milder third gate was opened for him: and he passed, not softly yet speedily, into that still country, where the hail-storms and fire-showers do not reach, and the heaviest-laden wayfarer at length lays down his load!

Contemplating this sad end of Burns, and how he sank unaided by any real help, uncheered by any wise sympathy, generous minds have sometimes figured to themselves, with a reproachful sorrow, that much might have been done for him; that by counsel, true affection and friendly ministrations, he might have been saved to himself and the world. We question whether there is not more tenderness of heart than soundness of judgment in these suggestions. It seems dubious to us whether the richest, wisest, most benevolent individual could have lent Burns any effectual help. Counsel, which seldom profits any one, he did not need; in his understanding, he knew the right from the wrong, as well perhaps as any man ever did; but the persuasion, which would have availed him, lies not so much in the head as in the heart, where no argument or expostulation could have assisted much to implant it. As to money again, we do not believe that this was his essential want; or well see how any private man could, even presupposing Burns's consent, have bestowed on him an independent fortune, with much prospect of decisive advantage. It is a mortifying truth, that two men in any rank of society, could hardly be found virtuous enough to give money, and to take it as a necessary gift, without injury to the moral entireness of one or both. But so stands the fact: Friendship, in the old heroic sense of that term, no longer exists; except in the cases of kindred or other legal affinity, it is in reality no longer expected, or recognized as a virtue among men. A close observer of manners has pronounced "Patronage," that is, pecuniary or other economic furtherance,[1] to be "twice [1] cursed;" cursing him that gives, and him that takes! And thus, in regard to outward matters also, it has become the rule, as in regard to inward it always was and must be the rule, that no one shall look for effectual help to another; but that each shall rest contented with what help he can afford himself. Such, we say, is the principle of modern Honor; naturally enough growing out of that sentiment of Pride, which we inculcate and encourage as the basis of our whole social morality. Many a poet has been poorer than Burns; but no one was ever prouder: we may question whether, without great precautions, even a pension from Royalty would not have galled and encumbered, more than actually assisted him.

Still less, therefore, are we disposed to join with another class of Burns's admirers, who accuse the higher ranks among us of having ruined Burns by their selfish neglect of him. We have already stated our doubts whether direct pecuniary help, had it been offered, would have been accepted, or could have proved very effectual. We shall readily admit, however, that much was to be done for Burns; that many a poisoned arrow might have been warded from his bosom; many an entanglement in his path cut asunder by the hand of the powerful; and light and heat, shed on him from high places, would have made his humble atmosphere more genial; and the softest heart then breathing might have lived and died with some fewer pangs. Nay, we shall grant farther, and for Burns it is granting much, that, with all his pride, he would have thanked, even with exaggerated gratitude, any one who had cordially befriended him: patronage, unless once cursed, needed not to have been twice so. At all events, the poor promotion he desired in his calling might have been granted: it was his own scheme, therefore likelier than any other to be of service. All this it might have been a luxury, nay it was a duty, for our nobility to have done. No part of all this, however, did any of them do; or apparently attempt, or wish to do: so much is granted against them. But what then is the amount of their blame? Simply that they were men of the world, and walked by the principles of such men; that they treated Burns, as other nobles and other commoners had done other poets; as the English did Shakspeare; as King Charles and his Cavaliers did Butler, as King Philip and his Grandees did Cervantes.[1] Do men gather grapes of thorns; or shall we cut down our thorns for yielding only a *fence* and haws?[2] How, indeed, could the "nobility and gentry of his native land" hold out any help to this "Scottish Bard, proud of his name and country"? Were the nobility and gentry[3] so much as able rightly to help themselves? Had they not their game to preserve; their borough interests to strengthen; dinners, therefore, of various kinds to eat and give? Were their means more than adequate to all this business, or less than adequate? Less than adequate, in general; few of them in reality were richer than Burns; many of them were poorer; for sometimes they had to wring their supplies, as with thumbscrews, from the hard hand; and, in their need of guineas, to forget their duty of mercy; which Burns was never reduced to do. Let us pity and forgive them. The game they preserved and shot, the dinners they ate and gave, the borough interests [1] they strengthened, the *little* Babylons [2] they severally builded by the glory of their might, are all melted or melting back into the primeval Chaos, as man's merely selfish endeavors are fated to do: and here was an action, extending, in virtue of its worldly influence, we may say, through all time; in virtue of its moral nature, beyond all time, being immortal as the Spirit of Goodness itself; this action was offered them to do, and light was not given them to do it. Let us pity and forgive them. But better than pity, let us go and *do otherwise*. Human suffering did not end with the life of Burns; neither was the solemn mandate, "Love one another, bear one another's burdens," given to the rich only, but to all men. True, we shall find no Burns to relieve, to assuage by our aid or our pity; but celestial natures, groaning under the fardels [3] of a weary life, we shall still find; and that wretchedness which Fate has rendered *voiceless* and *tuneless* is not the least wretched, but the most.

Still, we do not think that the blame of Burns's failure lies chiefly with the world. The world, it seems to us, treated him with more rather than with less kindness than it usually shows to such men. It has ever, we fear, shown but small favor to its Teachers: hunger and nakedness, perils and revilings, the prison, the cross, the poison-chalice have, in most times and countries, been the market-price it has offered for Wisdom, the welcome with which it has greeted those who have come to enlighten and purify it. Homer [1] and Socrates,[2] and the Christian Apostles, belong to old days; but the world's Martyrology was not completed with these. Roger Bacon [3] and Galileo [4] languish in priestly dungeons; Tasso [5] pines in the cell of a mad-house; Camoëns [6] dies begging on the streets of Lisbon. So neglected, so "persecuted they the Prophets,"[7] not in Judea only, but in all places where men have been. We reckon that every poet of Burns's order is, or should be, a prophet and teacher to his age; that he has no right to expect great kindness from it, but rather is bound to do it great kindness; that Burns, in particular, experienced fully the usual proportion of the world's goodness; and that the blame of his failure, as we have said, lies not chiefly with the world.

Where, then, does it lie? We are forced to answer: With himself; it is his inward, not his outward misfortunes that bring him to the dust. Seldom, indeed, is it otherwise; seldom is a life morally wrecked but the grand cause lies in some internal mal-arrangement, some want less of good fortune than of good guidance. Nature fashions no creature without implanting in it the strength needful for its action and duration; least of all does she so neglect her masterpiece and darling, the poetic soul. Neither can we believe that it is in the power of *any* external circumstances utterly to ruin the mind of a man; nay if proper wisdom be given him, even so much as to affect its essential health and beauty. The sternest sum-total of all worldly misfortunes is Death; nothing more *can* lie in the cup of human woe: yet many men, in all ages, have triumphed over Death, and led it captive; converting its physical victory into a moral victory for themselves, into a real and immortal consecration for all that their past life had achieved. What has been done, may be done again: nay, it is but the degree and not the kind of such heroism that differs in different seasons; for without some portion of this spirit, not of boisterous daring, but of silent fearlessness, of Self-denial in all its forms, no good man, in any scene or time, has ever attained to be good.

We have already stated the error of Burns; and mourned over it, rather than blamed it. It was the want of unity in his purposes, of consistency in his aims; the hapless attempt to mingle in friendly union the common spirit of the world with the spirit of poetry, which is of a far different and altogether irreconcilable nature. Burns was nothing wholly, and Burns could be nothing, no man formed as he was can be anything, by halves. The heart, not of a mere hot-blooded, popular Versemonger, or poetical *Restaurateur*,[1] but of a true Poet and Singer, worthy of the old religious heroic times, had been given him: and he fell in an age, not of heroism and religion, but of skepticism, selfishness and triviality, when true Nobleness was little understood, and its place supplied by a hollow, dissocial, altogether barren and unfruitful principle of Pride. The influences of that age, his open, kind, susceptible nature, to say nothing of his highly untoward situation, made it more than usually difficult for him to cast aside, or rightly subordinate; the better spirit that was within him ever sternly demanded its rights, its supremacy: he spent his life in endeavoring to reconcile these two; and lost it, as he must lose it, without reconciling them.

Burns was born poor; and born also to continue poor, for he would not endeavor to be otherwise: this it had been well could he have once for all admitted, and considered as finally settled. He was poor, truly; but hundreds even of his own class and order of minds have been poorer, yet have suffered nothing deadly from it: nay, his own Father had a far sorer battle with ungrateful destiny than his was; and he did not yield to it, but died courageously warring, and to all moral intents prevailing, against it. True, Burns had little means, had even little time for poetry, his only real pursuit and vocation; but so much the more precious was what little he had. In all these external respects his case was hard; but very far from the hardest. Poverty, incessant drudgery and much worse evils, it has often been the lot of Poets and wise men to strive with, and their glory to conquer. Locke[1] was banished as a traitor; and wrote his *Essay on the Human Understanding* sheltering himself in a Dutch garret. Was Milton rich or at his ease when he composed *Paradise Lost?* Not only low, but fallen from a height; not only poor, but impoverished; in darkness and with dangers compassed round, he sang his immortal song, and found fit audience,[1] though few. Did not Cervantes finish his work, a maimed soldier and in prison? Nay, was not the *Araucana,* which Spain acknowledges as its Epic, written without even the aid of paper; on scraps of leather, as the stout fighter and voyager snatched any moment from that wild warfare?

And what, then, had these men, which Burns wanted? Two things· both which, it seems to us, are indispensable for such men. They had a true religious principle of morals; and a single, not a double aim in their activity. They were not self-seekers and self-worshipers; but seekers and worshipers of something far better than Self. Not personal enjoyment was their object; but a high, heroic idea of Religion, of Patriotism, of heavenly Wisdom, in one or the other form, ever hovered before them; in which cause they neither shrank from suffering, nor called on the earth to witness it as something wonderful; but patiently endured, counting it blessedness enough so to spend and be spent. Thus the 'golden-calf of Self-love," however curiously carved, was not their Deity; but the Invisible Goodness, which alone is man's reasonable service. This feeling was as a celestial fountain, whose streams refreshed into gladness and beauty all the provinces of their otherwise too desolate existence. In a word, they willed one thing, to which all other things were subordinated and made subservient; and therefore they accomplished it. The wedge will rend rocks; but its edge must be sharp and single: if it be double, the wedge is bruised in pieces and will rend nothing.

Part of this superiority these men owed to their age; in which heroism and devotedness were still practiced, or at least not yet disbelieved in: but much of it likewise they owed to themselves. With Burns, again, it was different. His morality, in most of its practical points, is that of a mere worldly man; enjoyment, in a finer or coarser shape, is the only thing he longs and strives for. A noble instinct sometimes raises him above this; but an instinct only, and acting only for moments. He has no Religion; in the shallow age, where his days were cast, Religion was not discriminated from the New and Old Light *forms* of Religion; and was, with these, becoming obsolete in the minds of men. His heart, indeed, is alive with a trembling adoration, but there is no temple in his understanding. He lives in darkness and in the shadow of doubt. His religion, at best, is an anxious wish; like that of Rabelais,[1] "a great Perhaps."

He loved Poetry warmly, and in his heart; could he but have loved it purely, and with his whole undivided heart, it had been well. For Poetry, as Burns could have followed it, is but another form of Wisdom, of Religion; is itself Wisdom and Religion. But this also was denied him. His poetry is a stray vagrant gleam, which will not be extinguished within him, yet rises not to be the true light of his path, but is often a wildfire that misleads him. It was not necessary for Burns to be rich, to be, or to seem, "independent;" but it *was* necessary for him to be at one with his own heart; to place what was highest in his nature highest also in his life; "to seek within himself for that consistency and sequence, which external events would forever refuse him." He was born a poet; poetry was the celestial element of his being, and should have been the soul of his whole endeavors. Lifted into that serene ether, whither he had wings given him to mount, he would have needed no other elevation: poverty, neglect and all evil, save the desecration of himself and his Art, were a small matter to him; the pride and the passions of the world lay far beneath his feet; and he looked down alike on noble and slave, on prince and beggar, and all that wore the stamp of man, with clear recognition, with brotherly affection, with sympathy, with pity. Nay, we question whether for his culture as a Poet poverty and much suffering for a season were not absolutely advantageous. Great men, in looking back over their lives, have testified to that effect. "I would not for much," says Jean Paul,[1] "that I had been born richer." And yet Paul's birth was poor enough; for, in another place, he adds: "The prisoner's allowance is bread and water; and I had often only the latter." But the gold that is refined in the hottest furnace comes out the purest; or, as he has himself expressed it, "the canary-bird sings sweeter the longer it has been trained in a darkened cage."

A man like Burns might have divided his hours between poetry and virtuous industry; industry which all true feeling sanctions, nay prescribes, and which has a beauty, for that cause, beyond the pomp of thrones; but to divide his hours between poetry and rich man's banquets was an ill-starred and inauspicious attempt. How could he be at ease at such banquets? What had he to do there, mingling his music with the coarse roar of altogether earthly voices; brightening the thick smoke of intoxication with fire lent him from heaven? Was it his aim to *enjoy* life? To-morrow he must go drudge as an Exciseman! We wonder not that Burns became moody, indignant, and at times an offender against certain rules of society; but rather that he did not grow utterly frantic, and run *amuck* against them all. How could a man, so falsely placed, by his own or others' fault, ever know contentment or peaceable diligence for an hour? What he did, under such perverse guidance, and what he forbore to do, alike fill us with astonishment at the natural strength and worth of his character.

Doubtless there was a remedy for this perverseness; but not in others; only in himself; least of all in simple increase of wealth and worldly "respectability." We hope we have now heard enough about the efficacy of wealth for poetry, and to make poets happy. Nay have we not seen another instance of it in these very days? Byron, a man of an endowment considerably less ethereal than that of Burns, is born in the rank not of a Scottish plowman, but of an English peer:

the highest worldly honors, the fairest worldly career, are his by inheritance; the richest harvest of fame he soon reaps, in another province, by his own hand. And what does all this avail him? Is he happy, is he good, is he true? Alas, he has a poet's soul, and strives towards the Infinite and the Eternal; and soon feels that all this is but mounting to the house-top to reach the stars! Like Burns, he is only a proud man; might, like him, have "purchased [1] a pocket-copy of Milton to study the character of Satan;" for Satan also is Byron's grand exemplar, the hero of his poetry, and the model apparently of his conduct. As in Burns's case too, the celestial element will not mingle with the clay of earth; both poet and man of the world he must not be; vulgar Ambition will not live kindly with poetic Adoration; he *cannot* serve God and Mammon. Byron, like Burns, is not happy; nay he is the most wretched of all men. His life is falsely arranged: the fire that is in him is not a strong, still, central fire, warming into beauty the products of a world; but it is the mad fire of a volcano; and now— we look sadly into the ashes of a crater, which ere long will fill itself with snow!

Byron and Burns were sent forth as missionaries to their generation, to teach it a higher Doctrine, a purer Truth; they had a message to deliver, which left them no rest till it was accomplished; in dim throes of pain, this divine behest lay smouldering within them; for they knew not what it meant, and felt it only in mysterious anticipation, and they had to die without articulately uttering it. They are in the camp of the Unconverted; yet not as high messengers of rigorous though benignant truth, but as soft flattering singers, and in pleasant fellowship will they live there: they are first adulated, then persecuted; they accomplish little for others; they find no peace for themselves, but only death and the peace of the grave. We confess, it is not without a certain mournful awe that we view the fate of these noble souls, so richly gifted, yet ruined to so little purpose with all their gifts. It seems to us there is a stern moral taught in this piece of history,—*twice* told us in our own time! Surely to men of like genius, if there be any such, it carries with it a lesson of deep impressive significance. Surely it would become such a man, furnished for the highest of all enterprises, that of being the Poet of his Age, to consider well what it is that he attempts, and in what spirit he attempts it. For the words of Milton are true in all times, and were never truer than in this: "He[1] who would write heroic poems must make his whole life a heroic poem." If he cannot first so make his life, then let him hasten from this arena; for neither its lofty glories, nor its fearful perils, are fit for him. Let him dwindle into a modish balladmonger; let him worship and besing the idols of the time, and the time will not fail to reward him. If, indeed, he can endure to live in that capacity! Byron and Burns could not live as idol-priests, but the fire of their own hearts consumed them; and better it was for them that they could not. For it is not in the favor of the great or of the small, but in a life of truth, and in the inexpugnable citadel of his own soul, that a Byron's or a Burns's strength must lie. Let the great stand aloof from him, or know how to reverence him. Beautiful is the union of wealth with favor and furtherance for literature; like the costliest flower-jar enclosing the loveliest amaranth. Yet let not the relation be mistaken. A true poet is not one whom they can hire by money or flattery to be a minister of their pleasures, their writer of occasional verses, their purveyor of table-wit; he cannot be their menial, he cannot even be their partisan. At the peril of both parties, let no such union be attempted! Will a Courser of the Sun work softly in the harness of a Dray-horse? His hoofs are of fire, and his path is through the heavens, bringing light to all lands; will he lumber on mud highways, dragging ale for earthly appetites from door to door?

But we must stop short in these considerations, which would lead us to boundless lengths. We had something to say on the public moral character of Burns; but this also we must forbear. We are far from regarding him as guilty before the world, as guiltier than the average; nay from doubting that he is less guilty than one of ten thousand. Tried at a tribunal far more rigid than that where the *Plebiscita* [1] of common civic reputations are pronounced, he has seemed to us even there less worthy of blame than of pity and wonder. But the world is habitually unjust in its judgments of such men; unjust on many grounds, of which this one may be stated as the substance: It decides, like a court of law, by dead statutes; and not positively but negatively, less on what is done right, than on what is or is not done wrong. Not the few inches of deflection from the mathematical orbit, which are so easily measured, but the *ratio* of these to the whole diameter, constitutes the real aberration. This orbit may be a planet's, its diameter the breadth of the solar system; or it may be a city hippodrome; nay the circle of a ginhorse,[1] its diameter a score of feet or paces. But the inches of deflection only are measured: and it is assumed that the diameter of the ginhorse, and that of the planet, will yield the same ratio when compared with them! Here lies the root of many a blind, cruel condemnation of Burnses, Swifts,[2] Rousseaus,[3] which one never listens to with approval. Granted, the ship comes into harbor with shrouds and tackle damaged; the pilot is blameworthy; he has not been all-wise and all-powerful: but to know *how* blameworthy, tell us first whether his voyage has been round the Globe, or only to Ramsgate[4] and the Isle of Dogs.[5]

With our readers in general, with men of right feeling anywhere, we are not required to plead for Burns. In pitying admiration he lies enshrined in all our hearts, in a far nobler mausoleum than that one of marble; neither will his Works, even as they are, pass away from the memory of men. While the Shakspeares and Miltons roll on like mighty rivers through the country of Thought, bearing fleets of traffickers and assiduous pearl-fishers on their waves; this little Valclusa[1] Fountain will also arrest our eye: for this also is of Nature's own and most cunning workmanship, bursts from the depths of the earth, with a full gushing current, into the light of day; and often will the traveler turn aside to drink of its clear waters, and muse among its rocks and pines!

TO A MOUSE

ON TURNING HER UP IN HER NEST WITH THE PLOUGH, NOVEMBER, 1785

WEE, sleekit, cow'rin', tim'rous beastie,
O, what a panic's in thy breastie!
Thou need na start awa sae hasty,
   Wi' bickering brattle!
I wad be laith to rin an' chase thee,
   Wi' murdering pattle!

I'm truly sorry man's dominion
Has broken Nature's social union,
An' justifies that ill opinion
   Which makes thee startle
At me, thy poor earth-born companion,
   An' fellow-mortal!

I doubt na, whyles, but thou may thieve;
What then? poor beastie, thou maun live!
A daimen-icker in a thrave
   'S a sma' request:
I'll get a blessin' wi' the lave,
   And never miss 't!

Thy wee bit housie, too, in ruin!
Its silly wa's the win's are strewin'!
An' naething, now, to big a new ane,

O' foggage green!
An' bleak December's winds ensuin',
Baith snell an' keen!

Thou saw the fields laid bare an' waste,
And weary winter comin' fast,
And cozie here, beneath the blast,
Thou thought to dwell,
Till crash! the cruel coulter past
Out thro' thy cell.

That wee bit heap o' leaves an' stibble,
Has cost thee mony a weary nibble!
Now thou's turn'd out, for a' thy trouble,
But house or hald,
To thole the winter's sleety dribble,
An' cranreuch cauld!

But, Mousie, thou art no thy lane,
In proving foresight may be vain:
The best-laid schemes o' mice an' men,
Gang aft a-gley,
An' lea'e us nought but grief and pain,
For promis'd joy.

Still thou art blest, compared wi' me!
The present only toucheth thee:
But, och! I backward cast my e'e
On prospects drear!
An' forward, tho' I canna see,
I guess an' fear.

TO A MOUNTAIN DAISY

ON TURNING ONE DOWN WITH THE PLOUGH IN
APRIL, 1786

WEE, modest, crimson-tippèd flow'r,
Thou's met me in an evil hour;
For I maun crush amang the stoure
        Thy slender stem:
To spare thee now is past my pow'r,
        Thou bonnie gem.

Alas! it's no thy neebor sweet,
The bonnie lark, companion meet,
Bending thee 'mang the dewy weet,
        Wi' spreckl'd breast,
When upward-springing, blythe to greet
        The purpling east.

Cauld blew the bitter-biting north
Upon thy early, humble birth;
Yet cheerfully thou glinted forth
        Amid the storm,
Scarce rear'd above the parent earth
        Thy tender form.

The flaunting flow'rs our gardens yield,
High shelt'ring woods and wa's maun shield;
But thou, beneath the random bield

O' clod or stane,
Adorns the histie stibble-field,
Unseen, alane.

There, in thy scanty mantle clad,
Thy snawie bosom sun-ward spread,
Thou lifts thy unassuming head
In humble guise;
But now the share uptears thy bed,
And low thou lies!

Such is the fate of artless maid,
Sweet flow'ret of the rural shade,
By love's simplicity betray'd,
And guileless trust;
Till she, like thee, all soil'd, is laid
Low i' the dust.

Such is the fate of simple bard,
On life's rough ocean luckless starr'd!
Unskilful he to note the card
Of prudent lore,
Till billows rage, and gales blow hard,
And whelm him o'er!

Such fate to suffering Worth is giv'n,
Who long with wants and woes has striv'n,
By human pride or cunning driv'n
To mis'ry's brink,
Till, wrench'd of ev'ry stay but Heav'n,
He, ruin'd, sink!

Ev'n thou who mourn'st the Daisy's fate,
That fate is thine—no distant date;
Stern Ruin's plough-share drives elate,
    Full on thy bloom,
Till crush'd beneath the furrow's weight,
    Shall be thy doom!

HIGHLAND MARY

YE banks and braes and streams around
  The castle o' Montgomery,
Green be your woods, and fair your flowers,
  Your waters never drumlie!
There simmer first unfauld her robes,
  And there the langest tarry;
For there I took the last fareweel
  O' my sweet Highland Mary.

How sweetly bloom'd the gay green birk,
  How rich the hawthorn's blossom,
As underneath their fragrant shade
  I clasp'd her to my bosom!
The golden hours on angel wings
  Flew o'er me and my dearie;
For dear to me as light and life
  Was my sweet Highland Mary.

Wi' mony a vow and lock'd embrace
  Our parting was fu' tender;
And pledging aft to meet again,
  We tore oursels asunder;

But, O! fell Death's untimely frost,
    That nipt my flower sae early!
Now green's the sod and cauld's the clay,
    That wraps my Highland Mary!

O pale, pale now, those rosy lips,
    I aft hae kiss'd sae fondly!
And closed for aye the sparkling glance
    That dwelt on me sae kindly;
And mouldering now in silent dust
    That heart that lo'ed me dearly!
But still within my bosom's core
    Shall live my Highland Mary.

YE BANKS AND BRAES

Ye banks and braes o' bonnie Doon,
    How can ye bloom sae fair!
How can ye chant, ye little birds,
    And I sae fu' o' care!

Thou'll break my heart, thou bonnie bird,
    That sings upon the bough;
Thou minds me o' the happy days
    When my fause Luve was true.

Thou'll break my heart, thou bonnie bird,
    That sings beside thy mate;
For sae I sat, and sae I sang,
    And wist na o' my fate.

Aft hae I roved by bonnie Doon
  To see the woodbine twine,
And ilka bird sang o' its luve;
  And sae did I o' mine.

Wi' lightsome heart I pu'd a rose,
  Frae aff its thorny tree;
And my fause luver staw the rose,
  But left the thorn wi' me.

MY LUVE'S LIKE A RED, RED ROSE

O MY Luve's like a red, red rose
  That's newly sprung in June:
O my Luve's like the melodie
  That's sweetly play'd in tune.
As fair art thou, my bonnie lass,
  So deep in luve am I:
And I will luve thee still, my dear,
  Till a' the seas gang dry:

Till a' the seas gang dry, my dear,
  And the rocks melt wi' the sun;
I will luve thee still, my dear,
  While the sands o' life shall run.
And fare thee weel, my only Luve!
  And fare thee weel a while!
And I will come again, my Luve,
  Tho' it were ten thousand mile.

O, WERT THOU IN THE CAULD BLAST

O, WERT thou in the cauld blast,
  On yonder lea, on yonder lea,
My plaidie to the angry airt,
  I'd shelter thee, I'd shelter thee.
Or did misfortune's bitter storms
  Around thee blaw, around thee blaw,
Thy bield should be my bosom,
  To share it a', to share it a'.

Or were I in the wildest waste,
  Sae black and bare, sae black and bare,
The desert were a paradise,
  If thou wert there, if thou wert there.
Or were I monarch o' the globe,
  Wi' thee to reign, wi' thee to reign,
The brightest jewel in my crown
  Wad be my queen, wad be my queen.

SCOTS WHA HAE

ROBERT BRUCE'S ADDRESS TO HIS ARMY, BEFORE THE
BATTLE OF BANNOCKBURN

SCOTS, wha hae wi' Wallace bled,
Scots, wham Bruce has aften led,
Welcome to your gory bed,
  Or to victorie.

Now's the day, and now's the hour;
See the front o' battle lour!
See approach proud Edward's power—
    Chains and slaverie!

Wha will be a traitor knave?
Wha can fill a coward's grave?
Wha sae base as be a slave?
    Let him turn and flee!

Wha for Scotland's King and làw
Freedom's sword will strongly draw,
Freeman stand, or freeman fa'?
    Let him follow me!

By oppression's woes and pains!
By your sons in servile chains!
We will drain our dearest veins,
    But they shall be free!

Lay the proud usurpers low!
Tyrants fall in every foe!
Liberty's in every blow!
    Let us do or die!

AULD LANG SYNE

SHOULD auld acquaintance be forgot,
    And never brought to min'?
Should auld acquaintance be forgot,
    And auld lang syne?

For auld lang syne, my dear,
  For auld lang syne,
We'll tak a cup o' kindness yet,
  For auld lang syne.

We twa hae run about the braes,
  And pu'd the gowans fine;
But we've wander'd mony a weary foot
  Sin' auld lang syne.

We twa hae paidled i' the burn,
  From morning sun till dine;
But seas between us braid hae roar'd
  Sin' auld lang syne.

And there's a hand, my trusty fiere,
  And gie's a hand o' thine;
And we'll tak a right guid-willie waught,
  For auld lang syne.

And surely ye'll be your pint-stowp,
  And surely I'll be mine;
And we'll tak a cup o' kindness yet
  For auld lang syne.

NOTES

19, 1. Samuel Butler (1612-1680). The author of *Hudibras*, a witty satire on the Puritans. Praised for a time by Charles and his courtiers, he was permitted to die in poverty and neglect. He was "the glory and the scandal of the age," says Oldham.

2. Ask for bread, etc. Compare the original words, *Matthew*, vii, 9. It is related that Burns's widow, when informed of the "brave mausoleum" at Dumfries, remarked: "Poor Robbie, he asked for bread and they give him a stone."

3. Grand maxim. A principle of political economy, according to which the price of an article is regulated by supply and demand. As the supply of poetic genius is small, it ought to command a high price, that is, a generous recognition from the public, but does not always.

4. Spinning Jenny. A machine for spinning wool or cotton, invented in 1767 by James Hargreaves, an illiterate weaver of Lancashire. Carlyle implies that inventive genius, applied to material and commercial affairs, is generally rewarded liberally; but his illustration is not altogether a convincing one. Hargreaves was involved in disastrous lawsuits over his patents and died in moderate circumstances.

5. Brave mausoleum. This "huge, cumbrous, unsightly mausoleum," as Professor Shairp describes it, is in the corner of St. Michael's churchyard, Dumfries. It literally "shines" with its absurd tin-covered dome. The Burns Monument at Edinburgh is one of the most conspicuous objects in the city. Another "splendid monument" now stands near the poet's birthplace at Ayr, by the side of the "Auld Brig o' Doon."

6. John Gibson Lockhart. The son-in-law and biographer of Walter Scott. Carlyle's essay first appeared in the *Edinburgh Review*, in 1828, as a review of Lockhart's *Life of Robert Burns*.

20, 1. Sir Thomas Lucy. The proprietor of Charlecote Hall, near Stratford-on-Avon, in whose deer-park, according to the legend, Shakspeare was caught poaching. Having been arraigned before Sir Thomas, the young poacher, it is said, avenged himself by composing a satirical ballad upon the knight, and then fled to London to escape further prosecution.

2. **John-a-Combe.** A distinguished citizen of Stratford, the supposed subject of some satirical verses attributed to Shakspeare. His handsome tomb is near Shakspeare's grave, in Stratford Church.

3. **Excise Commissioners.** These were Burns's official superiors with whom he came in conflict on account of his sympathy with the democratic principles of the French Revolution. See note p. 82, 1.

4. **Caledonian Hunt.** An association composed of the chiefs of the northern aristocracy. Burns dedicated the first Edinburgh edition of his poems "To the noblemen and gentlemen of the Caledonian Hunt." These gentlemen had subscribed for one hundred copies of the *Poems* at a guinea a piece. The **Dumfries Aristocracy**, the fine people of Dumfries, were at first very friendly toward Burns, flattering him with attention, but finally drew away from him on account of his sympathy with the French and his dissipated habits.

5. **Ayr Writers.** Lawyers of the neighborhood (a lawyer in Scotland being called a *writer*), among whom was Robert Aiken, the friend of Burns to whom he dedicated "The Cotter's Saturday Night." The others, however, he regarded as a "merciless pack."

21, 1. **New and Old Light Clergy.** The church was divided into two hostile theological parties, the "New Lights," holding liberal or rationalistic views, and the "Auld Lights," the strict Calvinists. Burns engaged heartily in the fight, on the liberal side, satirizing the Auld Lights in the "Twa Herds," "Holy Willie's Prayer," and the "Holy Fair."

2. **James Currie.** A Scotch physician, best known for his valuable edition of Burns's Works, which he undertook for the benefit of the poet's widow and children, published in 1800. Josiah Walker's memoir of Burns was prefixed to a collection of his poems published in 1811.

22, 1. **Constable's Miscellany.** A series of popular works issued by Constable, the famous Edinburgh publisher who involved Scott in financial ruin.

23, 1. **Mr. Morris Birkbeck.** The author of *Notes on a Journey in America*, published in 1818.

NOTES

24, 1. Nine days. An allusion to the popular phrase, "nine days' wonder," which is thought to have originated in some reference to the nine days during which Lady Jane Grey was Queen of England.

25, 1. Titan. The Titans were fabled giants, sons and daughters of Uranus (Heaven) and Gæa (Earth). During their rebellion against Zeus they piled Mount Ossa upon Mount Pelion, in order to scale the walls of heaven.

26, 1. Robert Fergusson (1750-1774). A Scottish poet whom Burns greatly admired, and called his "elder brother in the muses." The monument over his grave in Edinburgh was erected by Burns. **Allan Ramsay** (1685-1758) was a Scottish poet, "at whose lamp Burns lighted his brilliant torch," says Scott. He reawakened in Scotland an interest in the native poetry.

27, 1. Sir Hudson Lowe. A British general, made governor of the island of St. Helena when Napoleon was sent there as an exile in 1815. He was much censured for his harsh treatment of the distinguished captive.

2. Amid the melancholy main. Quoted from Thomson's *Castle of Indolence*, i, 30. The following phrase in quotation marks is apparently one of Carlyle's manufactured quotations, alluding probably to Aristotle's famous theory that tragedy purifies the soul by a stage spectacle that arouses pity and fear in the beholder. Carlyle had a habit of quoting very loosely, his quotation marks sometimes being, like his capital letters, little more than marks of emphasis. "Eternal Melodies" for example, a few lines below, is a kind of stock phrase with him, like Emerson's "eternal verities."

28, 1. Thole the sleety dribble, etc. To endure the sleety drizzle and hoarfrost cold. From "To a Mouse."

2. It raises his thoughts, etc. : From Burns's *Commonplace Book*, where he speaks of a walk in the woods when the stormy wind is "howling among the trees and raving over the plain. It is my best season for devotion; my mind is rapt up in a kind of enthusiasm to Him who, in the pompous language of Scripture, 'walks on the wings of the wind.'"

29, 1. Arcadian illusion. Arcadia, in the center of the Peloponnesus, has been made by the poets the ideal home of pastoral simplicity, peace, and happiness.

30, 1. Æolian harp. The wind harp; from Æolus, the god of the winds. Usually an open box with strings stretched across it, which, placed in a draught of wind, produces sweet tones. This was a favorite simile with the writers of the period (see Burns's use of it, page 47 of this Essay), here probably adapted from Jean Paul Richter, the flowery German, whom Carlyle had carefully studied.

32, 1. **Si vis,** etc. *Si vis me flere, dolendum est primum ipsi tibi*—If you wish me to weep, you must mourn first yourself. Horace's *Ars Poetica*, 102.

33, 1. **Lord Byron** (1788-1824). The famous poet, whom Matthew Arnold couples with Wordsworth as "first and preeminent in actual performance, a glorious pair, among the English poets of this century." The allusions here are to the poems *Childe Harold, The Giaour,* and *Don Juan.* "In these poems," says Professor Beers, "there is a single figure—the figure of Byron under various masks—and one pervading mood, a restless and sardonic gloom, a weariness of life, a love of solitude, and a melancholy exaltation in the presence of the wilderness and the sea."

34, 1. **Affected.** Says Mr. Arnold: "Even of his passionate admirers, how many never got beyond the theatrical Byron, from whom they caught the fashion of deranging their hair, or of knotting their neck-handkerchief, or of leaving their shirt-collar unbuttoned; how few profoundly felt his vital influence, the influence of his splendid and imperishable excellence of sincerity and strength."

36, 1. **Mrs. Dunlop.** Burns's most valued friend and accomplished correspondent. Happening upon a copy of the first edition of his poems, she was charmed with "The Cotter's Saturday Night" and immediately sent a messenger to Burns, fifteen miles away, with a letter of praise and an order for several copies of the poems.

2. **Iron-mailed Epics, Virgins of the Sun,** etc. The prose and poetical romances of Scott, Byron, Moore, Southey, and other imaginative writers of the period were filled with the romanticism which Carlyle condemns. The world was searched for sensations.

38, 1. **Fifth act of a Tragedy.** A regularly constructed tragedy is always divided into five acts. In the fifth act the various elements of the plot are brought to their culmination in the death of the hero or heroine.

2. **Vates.** The Latin word for *poet;* literally, a foreteller, soothsayer.

3. **Delphi.** The seat of the famous oracle of Apollo, the god of music and poetry; situated at the foot of Mount Parnassus, the home of the Muses. Here also was the

NOTES

Castalian spring, which was supposed to give inspiration to those who drank its waters.

4. Minerva Press. A printing establishment famous in London about a century ago for its trashy, ultra-sentimental, "rose-colored" novels, with absurd plots laid "somewhere near the moon."

39, 1. Dan to Beersheba. Dan was the most northern and Beersheba the most southern city of the Holy Land. Hence the meaning, from one end of the kingdom to the other; everywhere. Like this is the English phrase "From John o' Groat's to Land's End."

2. Borgia. An Italian family of the fifteenth century, celebrated for its monstrous crimes.

3. Martin Luther (1483–1546). The great religious leader of the German Reformation. His nature was passionate and violent, and his righteous wrath often discharged itself in thunder and lightning against the abuses of Rome.

4. Mossgiel. The farm where Burns made his first disastrous experiment in farming, and where he wrote many of his finest poems. **Tarbolton** was a town of Ayrshire where Burns lived, on the farm of Lochlea, from his seventeenth to his twenty-fourth year.

5. Crockford's. A famous gaming club-house in London, opened in 1849; so called from the proprietor. It was for a time the center of fashionable gambling, and numbered the Duke of Wellington among its original members. The **Tuileries** was a royal palace in Paris, begun in 1564 by Catharine de Medici and finished by Louis XIV. It was burned by the Communists in 1871.

40, 1. Cobweb speculations. Carlyle seems to have in mind Macaulay's *Essay on Milton*, that had appeared three years before, in which the brilliant author maintained the paradoxical proposition that poetry declines as civilization advances.

2. Druids. The religious order of the ancient Britons; they exercised the functions of judge, bard, prophet, and priest.

3. Theocritus. A Greek poet of Syracuse who lived about 270 B.C., distinguished as the father of pastoral poetry, especially of that form known as the idyl, in which simple country scenes and the happy life of shepherds and shepherdesses were presented. A good example of the modern idyl is "The Cotter's Saturday Night," or Goldsmith's "The Deserted Village."

4. Holy Fair. In this poem, in which *Superstition*,

Hypocrisy, and *Fun* are characters, Burns satirizes the abuses connected with the rural gathering for the celebration of the Holy Communion, a kind of Scotch campmeeting.

5. **Council of Trent.** A celebrated council of the Roman Catholic Church, opened in 1545, for the purpose of reconciliation between Protestants and the Pope. Under the influence of the Jesuits the creed of the Church was made more rigid, and the hope of reconciliation removed forever.

6. **Roman Jubilee.** A church celebration at Rome, every twenty-fifth year, when extraordinary indulgences are granted to the faithful.

42, 1. **Burin.** The instrument used by engravers for cutting the design upon steel or copper. **Moritz Retzsch** (1779–1857) was a German painter and designer, famous for his etchings illustrating Goethe's *Faust*.

2. **Boreas**, the north wind; *doure*, stubborn; *Phœbus*, Apollo, the sun-god; *gies, etc.*, gives us a short-lived stare; *lift*, the sky; *ae night*, one night; *burns, etc.*, streams with snowy wreaths choked up; *bocked*, belched.

43, 1. **The Auld Brig.** Two bridges cross the Ayr, in the town of Ayr. The erection of the New Brig is celebrated in the poem "The Brigs of Ayr." The Auld Brig is still used by foot-passengers.

2. **Thowes**, thaws; *snaw-broo rowes*, melted snow rolls; *spate*, flood; *Glenbuck*, the source of the river Ayr; *Rattonkey*, a small landing-place near the town; *gumlie jaups*, muddy splashes.

3. **Poussin-picture.** Nicolas Poussin (1594–1665) was a celebrated French painter, called the "Raphael of France," and regarded by Ruskin as "the principal master of the classical landscape."

4. **Homer's smithy,** etc. Carlyle's memory was confused here. The famous description of the adventure of Ulysses in the cave of the Cyclops Polyphemus, *Odyssey*, Bk. ix, would serve as an example of "clearness and minute fidelity;" but it is Virgil who describes the *Smithy* of the Cyclopes under Mt. Ætna, *Æneid*, viii, 407–453. This idea is borrowed from Hesiod's *Theogony*, in which the Cyclopes are represented as giant smiths who forge the thunderbolts for Zeus. The description of the **Yoking of Priam's Chariot** is in the *Iliad*, Bk. xxiv.

44, 1. **Samuel Richardson** (1689–1761). The first great English novelist, author of *Pamela, Clarissa Harlowe*, and, *Sir Charles Grandison*. **Daniel Defoe** (1661–1731) was the celebrated author of *Robinson Crusoe, History of the London Plague*, and some two hundred other works.

45, 1. **Red-wat-shod.** Red-wet-shod, that is, with bloodstained feet.

2. **Dugald Stewart** (1753–1828). The eminent Professor of Moral Philosophy in the University of Edinburgh. The quotation is from a letter printed in Dr. Currie's edition of the *Works of Burns*, to which Carlyle frequently alludes in the essay.

3. **John Keats** (1795–1821). Author of *Hyperion, Lamia* and *Eve of St. Agnes*. This unappreciative criticism suggests Carlyle's characterization of Shelley as "a kind of ghastly object, colorless, pallid, without health, or warmth, or vigor." For Carlyle there could be no beauty without force.

46, 1. **Hell of Dante.** Dante's great poem, the *Divina Commedia* (Divine Comedy), is divided into three parts, *Inferno* (Hell), *Purgatorio* (Purgatory), and *Paradiso* (Paradise). The poet depicts a vision in which he is conducted by Virgil through the ten circles of Hell, where he witnesses "all the woe of all the universe;" then through Purgatory, and then, by Beatrice, through Paradise.

2. **Novum Organum.** Bacon's great philosophical work, the "new method," by which human knowledge should be increased.

47, 1. **Passage above quoted.** He means, of course, the letter from which the passage is quoted.

49, 1. **Ourie cattle,** shivering cattle; *wha bide,* etc., who endure this race; *deep-lairing, sprattle,* deep-wading, struggle; *scaur,* barren bank, or mountain side; *ilk happing,* each hopping; *chittering,* trembling with cold. The passage is from the poem, "A Winter Night."

2. **Wad,** would; *men,* mend; *aiblins,* perhaps; *dinna ken,* do not know; *wae,* sorrowful. From "Address to the Deil."

50, 1. **Dr. Slop and Uncle Toby.** Characters in Sterne's *Tristram Shandy.*

2. **Indignation makes verses.** From Juvenal's *Satires,* i, 79; *Facit indignatio versum.*

3. **Dr. Samuel Johnson** (1709–1784). Author of the famous Dictionary, the *Rambler,* and *Rasselas.* His words were, "Sir, I like a good hater." See Boswell's *Life of Johnson.*

51, 1. **Dweller in yon dungeon dank.** The first line of the "Ode, Sacred to the Memory of Mrs. Oswald."

2. **Furies of Æschylus.** The Furies were the goddesses of vengeance. The allusion is to the chorus of Furies in the *Eumenides*, one of the tragedies of Æschylus, the greatest Greek dramatic poet.

3. **Darkness visible.** Milton's *Paradise Lost*, i, 62.

52, 1. **Macpherson's Farewell.** Macpherson was a Highland freebooter, of great strength and musical taste. While lying in prison he composed his "Farewell," words and air, and when brought to the gallows played it, and then broke his violin across his knee. Burns's chorus, "Sae rantingly, sae wantonly," etc., is an adaptation of Macpherson's words.

2. **Cacus.** A mighty robber giant who lived in a cave on Mount Aventine in Italy. He stole some oxen from Hercules and dragged them into his cave by their tails, to deceive the hero by the tracks as to the direction taken; but, being discovered by the bellowing of the cattle, he was strangled by the enraged hero. See Virgil's *Æneid*, viii, 190-270.

3. **Sturt.** Disturbance, or molestation.

4. **Nimrod.** The mighty hunter. See *Genesis*, x, 8-11, and 1 *Chronicles*, i, 10.

5. **Thebes.** The capital of Bœotia, the scene of some of the great Greek tragedies, the *Seven against Thebes* of Æschylus, the *Œdipus Tyrannus* of Sophocles, and others. **Pelops's line** is an allusion to the tragedies of Æschylus on the subject of the murder of Agamemnon, a descendant of Pelops, King of Pisa in Elis, who gave his name to Peloponnesus. Compare Milton's lines in "Il Penseroso" on "gorgeous Tragedy," "presenting Thebes, or Pelops' line."

6. **Material Fate.** The fundamental idea in the Greek tragedies is fate, destiny, or Nemesis.

53, 1. **Laurence Sterne** (1713-1768). Author of the famous novels, *Tristram Shandy* and *The Sentimental Journey*. Carlyle elsewhere speaks of him as "our best specimen of humor, with all his faults; our finest, if not our strongest."

54, 1. **Ludwig Tieck** (1773-1853). A German poet and novelist, especially famous for his fantastic tales, and his translation of Shakspeare. **Karl August Musäus** (1735-1787) was a German writer of humorous and satirical works, author of *Popular Legends of Germany* and *Friend Hein's Apparitions, in Holbein's Manner*.

2. **Tophet.** Originally a place near Jerusalem in the valley of Gehenna, where fire was kept perpetually burning

NOTES

to destroy the dead bodies, bones, and filth deposited there; hence the derived meaning, hell.

55, 1. Raucle carlin. A fearless old woman. The scene of the poem is laid at the ale-house of Poosie-Nansie.

56, 1. David Teniers (1582–1649). A famous Flemish painter. His subjects were mainly from tavern scenes and low life. His son was a still greater painter.

2. Beggars' Opera. The first English ballad opera, written by John Gay, and first acted at Lincoln's Inn Fields, London, in 1727. Beggars' Bush was a comedy by Francis Beaumont, written in 1661.

3. Cantata. A musical composition composed of solos and choruses, dramatically arranged. Burns uses the word as a sub-title to "The Jolly Beggars."

57, 1. Osorius. A learned Portuguese bishop, called the "Cicero of Portugal," for the purity of his Latin style. Among his famous works is an "Address to Queen Elizabeth, on the True Faith." The quotation is from Bacon's *Advancement of Learning*, Bk. i.

2. Limbo. According to mediæval theology, a place on the confines of Paradise, for those who cannot be admitted into Paradise, either because they have never heard the gospel or have never been baptized. Milton (*Paradise Lost*, iii, 448) makes it the "Fools' Paradise," a place for idiots, madmen, and others not responsible for their sins.

3. Debatable land. A strip of land between the rivers Esk and Sark was long claimed by both Scotland and England, and thus came to be known as the debatable land. Hence the figurative meaning, a vague, uncertain region of thought.

4. Venus rose, etc. In Greek mythology, Venus (Aphrodite) is represented as having sprung from the foam of the sea.

58, 1. Fletcher's aphorism. Andrew Fletcher, a Scottish orator and member of the Scottish Parliament, in a letter to the Marquis of Montrose: "I knew a very wise man who believed that, if a man were permitted to make all the ballads, he need not care who should make the laws of a nation."

59, 1. Grays and Glovers. Thomas Gray (1716–1771), author of the "Elegy written in a Country Churchyard." Richard Glover (1712–1785), author of "Leonidas." Both poets were distinguished for classical scholarship.

2. In vacuo. In empty space.

60, 1. Oliver Goldsmith (1728–1774). Goldsmith, in his

"Traveller" and "The Deserted Village," was one of the first to break away from the classical affectation of Pope's school, and introduce nature and humanity into poetry.

2. **Rambler.** A series of periodical essays in the form of Addison's *Spectator*. *Rasselas, Prince of Abyssinia* is a prose romance; the thought is English, but the scenery is oriental.

3. **Joseph Addison** (1672–1719), **Richard Steele** (1671–1729). This celebrated literary partnership began in 1709 with the *Tatler*, issued three times a week, which was followed in 1711 by the *Spectator*, issued daily.

4. **Thomas Boston** (1676–1732). A Scottish Calvinistic divine, published his *Human Nature in its Fourfold State* in 1720.

5. **Jacobite blood.** The adherents of the dethroned James II and his descendants were called Jacobites; Lat. *Jacobus*, James. They were powerful in Scotland, and twice rose in unsuccessful revolt.

6. **Lord Kames.** Henry Home (1696–1782), a Scottish judge. His chief work, *Elements of Criticism*, received the praise of Dr. Johnson, who hated Scotchmen on principle.

7. **David Hume** (1711–1776). Author of the celebrated *History of England* and of important philosophical essays.

William Robertson (1721–1793) was an eminent historian, author of the *History of Scotland* and the *History of the Emperor Charles V*. **Adam Smith** (1723–1790) was a philosopher and political economist, author of *Theory of Moral Sentiments* and *The Wealth of Nations*; sometimes called the "father of political economy."

61, 1. **Jean Racine** (1639–1699). A French dramatic poet, whom Hallam thought to be "next to Shakspeare among all the moderns," and "second only to Virgil among all poets."

2. **Voltaire** (1694–1778). French poet, critic, historian, and philosopher, "the sovereign writer of his century." His writings are brilliant, satirical and skeptical.

3. **Charles Batteux** (1713–1780). A professor of Greek and Latin philosophy in the College of France, and author of a *Treatise on the Fine Arts*.

4. **Nicholas Boileau** (1636–1711). A French poet and satirist, and highest literary authority of his age. His *Art of Poetry* was modeled from Horace, and became the model for Pope and his school in England.

5. **Montesquieu** (1689–1755). A French philosopher.

His principal work, *Spirit of Laws*, was one of the first to place the study of history and politics upon a philosophical basis.

6. **Gabriel Bonnot de Mably** (1709-1785). A French publicist and historical writer. He was consulted by the framers of the Constitution of the United States, and he embodied his views in his *Observations on the Government of the United States of America.*

7. **François Quesnay** (1694-1774). A French physician and political economist, chief exponent of the doctrine of *Laissez faire* (Let things take their own course).

8. **La Fleche.** A town on the Loire, where Hume lived while writing his *Treatise on Human Nature.*

62, 1. **Doctrine of Rent.** A discussion in Adam Smith's *Wealth of Nations.* David Hume, the historian, wrote *Dialogues Concerning the Natural History of Religion.*

2. **Propaganda.** A society established at Rome for the management of the Roman Catholic missions (Societas de Propaganda Fide).

63, 1. **Symbol dear.** The thistle is the national emblem of Scotland. **Bear** is barley. The quotation is from the poem, "To the Guidwife of Wauchope House."

2. **Intercalated.** Inserted; Lat. *inter*, between, and *calare*, to call.

65, 1. **Rock of Independence.** An expression that occurs in a letter to Miss Davies, in which Burns says much about "the inequalities of life" and "the capricious distinctions of fortune." In spite of the noble sentiments of his "A man's a man for a' that." Burns sometimes did "hang his head, for honest poverty," with an embittered feeling of jealousy toward people of wealth and rank. In a letter to Mr. Erskine he speaks humorously of the "fanfaronade of independence to be found in his works." Compare p. 81, l. 28.

67, 1. **Crossing of a brook.** An allusion to Cæsar's crossing the Rubicon, a little stream dividing ancient Gaul from Italy. This act was virtually a declaration of war against the Republic and the beginning of Imperial Rome.

68, 1. **Priest-like father.** See "The Cotter's Saturday Night," stanzas 12-14.

2. **In glory,** etc. Quoted, incorrectly, from Wordsworth's "Leech-Gatherer, or Resolution and Independence." The lines refer directly to Burns:

> Of him who walked in glory and in joy,
> Following his plough, along the mountain side.

71, 1. Passions raging like demons. Loosely quoted from Burns's letter to Dr. Moore.
2. Hungry Ruin has him in the wind. From the letter to Dr. Moore. Ruin, like a hungry wolf, follows his scent with a favoring wind.
3. Farewell to Scotland. Burns had decided to emigrate to America. He says: "I had taken the last farewell of my few friends; my chest was on the road to Greenock; and I had composed the last song I should ever measure in Caledonia,—'The gloomy night is gathering fast,'—when a letter from Dr. Blacklock to a friend of mine overthrew all my schemes, by opening new prospects to my poetic ambition." Dr. Thomas Blacklock was a divine and poet in Edinburgh, to whom a copy of Burns's poems had been sent.
72, 1. Mockery King: "Oh, that I were a mockery king of snow!" *Richard II*, Act iv, i, 260.
2. Rienzi. An eloquent Roman tribune, who, becoming intoxicated with power, "degenerated," says Gibbon, "into the vices of a king," and was driven from the city by the people, and finally assassinated in 1354.
74, 1. Virgilium vidi tantum. I have almost seen Virgil. Ovid's *Tristia*, iv, x, 51.
2. Professor Ferguson. Adam Ferguson, who preceded Dugald Stewart in the professorship of philosophy in the University of Edinburgh.
3. Henry William Bunbury. A commonplace artist of the period.
75, 1. John Langhorne (1735-1779). A forgotten English poet, chiefly known for his translation of Plutarch's *Lives*.
2. Mr. Nasmyth's picture. This portrait, painted when the poet was about twenty-six years old, is the only authentic likeness of Burns.
3. Douce gudeman. Thrifty good man.
76, 1. In malam partem. In bad part, disparagingly.
78, 1. Dr. Thomas Blacklock. A blind poet of Edinburgh, whose kindly letter received just as he was about to sail for Jamaica changed the whole fortune of Burns's life.
79, 1. Excise and Farm scheme. Burns now rented the farm of Ellisland, about five miles from Dumfries, but depended more confidently upon his appointment as an Excise officer.
2. Gauge. Burns's duties as an Exciseman required him

to gauge, or measure, the contents of barrels of whisky, the principal article upon which the excise tax was levied. This occupation, though respectable enough, kept him in an unfortunate association with his worst enemy.

3. **Lie at the pool.** An allusion to the miraculous pool of Bethesda, *John* v, 2-9.

4. **Spirit of Patronage.** Hitherto it had been the custom for literary men to obtain assistance or patronage from some wealthy or influential person, to whom their publications would be dedicated. Burns scorned this method of gain. While inscribing "The Cotter's Saturday Night" to Robert Aiken, he says:

> No mercenary bard his homage pays;
> With honest pride I scorn each selfish end;
> My dearest meed, a friend's esteem and praise.

81, 1. Picturesque tourists. To these words Carlyle appends this note: "There is one little sketch by certain 'English gentlemen' of this class, which, though adopted in Currie's *Narrative*, and since then repeated in most others, we have all along felt an invincible disposition to regard as imaginary: 'On a rock that projected into the stream, they saw a man employed in angling, of a singular appearance. He had a cap made of fox-skin on his head, a loose greatcoat fixed round him by a belt, from which depended an enormous Highland broad-sword. It was Burns.' Now, we rather think, it was *not* Burns. For, to say nothing of the fox-skin cap, the loose and quite Hibernian watchcoat with the belt, what are we to make of this 'enormous Highland broad-sword' depending from him? More especially, as there is no word of parish constables on the outlook to see whether, as Dennis phrases it, he had an eye to his own midriff or that of the public! Burns, of all men, had the least need, and the least tendency, to seek for distinction, either in his own eyes, or those of others, by such poor mummeries."

2. **Mæcenas.** A wealthy Roman nobleman, and patron of Virgil, Horace and other men of genius. His name has become proverbial for a liberal patron of letters.

82, 1. Collision, etc. Burns warmly sympathized with the French revolutionists, and sent to the French Convention a present of some guns, which he had taken from a smuggling brig, in the performance of his duties as Exciseman. This led the Board of Excise to order an inquiry into his political conduct.

83, 1. Cast the first Stone. See *John,* viii, 7.

2. Jacobin. The most violent party among the French revolutionists; so called from their place of meeting, the monastery of St. Jacques.

3. Grocerdom and grazierdom. Shopkeepers and farmers; a characteristic Carlyle expression.

84, 1. Lady Grizzel Baillie. A Scottish poet who died in 1746. The ballad is generally entitled "Werena my heart light, I wad dee." *Ance,* once; *fu',* full; *ane,* one; *hing,* hang; *dowie,* sad; *corn-bing,* corn-heap; *linking,* tripping; *werena,* were not.

2. Where bitter indignation, etc. The epitaph upon the grave of Dean Swift, composed by himself—*Ubi sæva indignatio cor ulterius lacerare nequit.*

85, 1. If he entered, etc. Quoted from Lockhart's *Life of Burns,* ch. vii.

2. Spurned all other reward. To James Johnson's *Musical Museum* Burns "gratuitously contributed not less than one hundred and eighty-four songs, original, altered, or collected," says Prof. Shairp. His very last work was contributing to a similar collection published by George Thomson, to whom he wrote: "As to remuneration, you may think my songs either above or below price; for they shall be absolutely the one or the other. In the honest enthusiasm with which I embark in your undertaking, to talk of money, wages, fee, hire, etc., would be downright prostitution of soul."

3. Thoughtless follies. From "A Bard's Epitaph:"

> But thoughtless follies laid him low,
> And stained his name.

4. Volunteer. Perhaps to atone somewhat for his political offenses, Burns enlisted in a corps of volunteers at Dumfries, and composed the spirited patriotic song, "Does haughty Gaul invasion threat?" which became at once popular.

87, 1. Economic furtherance. A Carlyleism for material assistance.

88, 1. Twice cursed, etc. A play upon Portia's words in her speech upon the quality of mercy, *The Merchant of Venice,* iv, i, 196.

89, 1. Cervantes (1547–1616). A celebrated Spanish writer, author of *Don Quixote.* He was wounded in the battle of Lepanto, and later was seized by an Algerine corsair and held for some years as a slave, and he was several times lodged in prison on civil prosecutions.

2. **Haws.** The fruit of the hawthorn, commonly used in England for *fence* hedges. The scriptural allusion is to *Matthew*, vii, 16.

3. **Nobility and gentry**, etc. Loosely quoted from the dedication of the Edinburgh edition of the *Poems*, 1787.

90,1. **Borough interests** would be called in America "village politics."

2. **Little Babylon.** Babylon, the proudest and most glorious city of antiquity, crumbled to ruins about the beginning of the Christian era.

3. **Fardels.** Literally, bundles or packs. Compare *Hamlet*, iii, 1:

Who would fardels bear,
To grunt and sweat under a weary life.

91, 1. **Homer.** The great epic poet of Greece, author of the *Iliad* and *Odyssey*. He is supposed to have lived about 800 B.C., and according to tradition was a poor, blind minstrel who traveled about singing his poems in separate parts, which were woven together by some later poet.

2. **Socrates.** The wisest philosopher of antiquity. He was condemned to drink the fatal hemlock, on the charge that he disbelieved the gods of his country and corrupted the Athenian youth with his teachings.

3. **Roger Bacon** (1214?-1292?). An English monk, regarded as the greatest scholar of the thirteenth century. His *Opus Majus*, an important contribution to science, was condemned by the church, and the author confined ten years in prison.

4. **Galileo** (1564-1642). The illustrious Italian philosopher, and inventor of the telescope. For his advocacy of the Copernican theory of the earth's motion, he was summoned before the Inquisition at Rome, made to abjure his heresies, condemned to be imprisoned during the Pope's pleasure, and to recite once a week for three years the seven penitential Psalms.

5. **Torquato Tasso** (1544-1595). A famous Italian epic poet, author of *Jerusalem Delivered*. He was imprisoned by Alfonso, Duke of Ferrara, and by his orders treated as a madman. The cause is involved in mystery.

6. **Camoëns** (1524?-1579). The most celebrated Portuguese poet, author of *The Lusiad*, a heroic poem in which, says Mme. de Staël, "The national glory of the Portuguese

is illustrated under all the forms that imagination can devise."

7. **Persecuted they the prophets.** *Matthew*, v, 12.

92, 1. Restaurateur. One who refreshes or restores. The keeper of a place of refreshment or amusement. This may be a contemptuous fling at Scott, whom Carlyle once called "the great intellectual restaurateur of Europe."

93, 1. John Locke (1632–1704). A celebrated English philosopher. Being intimately associated with Shaftesbury, the Lord Chancellor, who was charged with high treason, he fled to Holland for safety, but returned upon the completion of the Revolution in 1689.

94, 1. Found fit audience, etc. See *Paradise Lost*, vii, 26–31:

> On evil days though fallen, and evil tongues,
> In darkness, and with dangers compassed round,
> And solitude. . . . Still govern thou my song,
> Urania, and fit audience find, though few.

2. **Araucana.** An epic poem in thirty-seven cantos, by Alonso de Ercilla (1530?–1600?). It recounts the poet's adventures while engaged in the Spanish expedition against Arauco, in South America, and was written, he says, in the wilderness, where he fought, on scraps of paper and skins.

95, 1. François Rabelais (1490?–1553?). A French satirist, whose great work, *Gargantua and Pantagruel*, assails all classes of society, but especially the monks. Sometimes called the "Comic Homer."

96, 1. Jean Paul Friedrich Richter (1763–1825). A popular, witty, and wise German writer, usually called simply Jean Paul: Carlyle first introduced him to English readers in 1827, with an essay on his genius. Best known in English by his "Flower, Fruit, and Thorn Pieces."

98, 1. Purchased a pocket-copy of Milton, etc. From a letter to William Nicol: "I have bought a pocket Milton, which I carry perpetually about with me, in order to study the sentiments—the dauntless magnanimity, the intrepid, unyielding independence, the desperate daring, and noble defiance of hardship, in that great personage, Satan."

99, 1. He who would write, etc. Quoted, in Carlyle's characteristically free manner, from the *Apology for Smectymnuus*. The original reads: "He who would not be frustrate of his hope to write well hereafter in laudable things ought himself to be a true poem."

100, 1. Plebiscita. Lat. pl. of *plebiscitum; plebs,* people, and *scitum,* decree. Hence, a decision by the people, as opposed to one by the senate or ruling body. Carlyle is comparing the popular judgment of Burns with the sympathetic, appreciative judgment of his own heart and unprejudiced mind.

101, 1. Ginhorse. Mill horse, one that turns a mill by going perpetually around in a small circle.

2. Jonathan Swift (1667–1745). Author of the famous *Gulliver's Travels* and the bitterest and strongest satirist in our literature. See note, p. 84, 2.

3. Jean Jacques Rousseau (1712–1778). A brilliant French writer, whose political and social speculations were widely influential and mischievous. His *Confessions* reveals a man in whom genius and wickedness were strangely mingled.

4. Ramsgate. A popular resort on the southeast coast of England.

5. Isle of Dogs. A peninsula of the Thames, where formerly the King's hounds were kept, now occupied by the West India docks.

102, 1. Valclusa. A romantic valley near Avignon, where the Italian poet Petrarch secluded himself for several years. In these closing lines Carlyle associates, very beautifully, but perhaps not so justly, from a critical point of view, the fame of Burns with that of Petrarch.

TOPICS FOR STUDY AND DISCUSSION

1. What was the occasion of the writing of this *Essay on Burns?*
2. What were Carlyle's ideas as to the characteristics of a good biography? (Pages 21-24.)
3. What can you say of the popularity of Burns's poems, in his lifetime? At the present time? What are some of the reasons for their popularity?
4. What do you think are the "enduring qualities" of his poems? (Page 31.)
5. What was Carlyle's opinion of romantic novels? Why is our interest in them usually transient? (Pages 36, 37.)
6. Name some writers who have taken their subjects from the life about them. From humble country life. From imaginary and foreign life.
7. Tell something of Burns's power of description. (Page 42.) Select your own illustrations from his poems.
8. From what Carlyle writes, can you suggest some of the "Shakspearean qualities" in Burns? (Page 54.)
9. Can you find good reason to agree with Carlyle's estimate of the excellence and the lasting popularity of the songs of Burns? (Pages 56-59.)
10. What does Carlyle say of the literature of Scotland and the influence of Burns on it? (Pages 59-63.)
11. Tell something about other Scottish writers whom you know.
12. Study and explain what Carlyle says of man's attitude towards Necessity on pages 69, 70.
13. What effects did early environment and education have on Burns?
14. Discuss Burns's life in Edinburgh, making clear the circumstances of his going to Edinburgh, the manner of his life while there, and the effect that this life had on him.

TOPICS FOR STUDY AND DISCUSSION   131

15. To what extent may we regard Burns's life a failure? Where, according to Carlyle, does the blame for Burns's failure lie?
16. What reasons can you see for forming a charitable judgment of the life of Burns?
17. Carlyle contrasts Burns's life with that of Milton and other great writers who also were poor and unfortunate. In what respects was Burns weaker than these others?
18. What does Carlyle consider "the error" of Burns? (Pages 92, 96.)
19. Study the sentence about the wedge at the top of page 95. What is the meaning?
20. Does Carlyle consider wealth an advantage to a writer? How can poverty be an advantage? (Page 96.)
21. What do you think of this Essay as a whole?
22. Compare the Essay with Carlyle's theory of a good biography. (Pages 21-24.)
23. Select two or three paragraphs that show Carlyle's characteristics as a writer. Name some of his chief characteristics.
24. Give a short account of Carlyle's life and his writings.
25. Give the titles of six familiar poems of Burns. Describe some of the poems which you have read.

GLOSSARY

Aft. Often.
A-gley. Off the right line; wrong.
Auld lang syne. (Old, long, since) the long ago.
Bickering brattle. Trembling flight.
Bield. Shelter.
Big. Build.
Birk. Birch.
Braes. Slopes of a hill.
Burn. Stream.
But. Without.
Card. Chart or compass card.
Coulter. A knife attached to a plough for cutting the sod.
Cranreuch. Hoar-frost.
Diamen-icker. An occasional ear of corn.
Drumlie. Muddy.
Fiere. Companion.
Foggage. Coarse grass.
Fu'. Full.
Gang. Go.
Gowan. Daisy.

Guid-willie. Hearty.
Hald. An abiding-place.
Histie. Dry; barren.
Ilka. Every.
Laith. Loath; reluctant.
Lave. The rest; the others.
Maun. Must.
Meet. Suitable; fit.
Na. Not.
No thy lane. Not alone.
Pattle. A plough-staff, or small spade (paddle), used for cleaning the plough.
Silly. Weak.
Sleekit. Sly.
Snell. Biting.
Staw. Stole.
Stoure. Dust.
Thole. Suffer; endure.
Thrave. Twenty-four sheaves of corn.
Wad. Would.
Wa's. Walls.
Waught. A big drink.
Weet. Rain; wetness.
Whyles. Sometimes.

www.ingramcontent.com/pod-product-compliance
Lightning Source LLC
LaVergne TN
LVHW011205080426
835508LV00007B/605